SEXUALITY AND SEVERE AUTISM

A PRACTICAL GUIDE FOR PARENTS, CAREGIVERS AND HEALTH EDUCATORS

Kate E. Reynolds

Jessica Kingsley *Publishers*
London and Philadelphia

First published in 2014
by Jessica Kingsley Publishers
73 Collier Street
London N1 9BE, UK
and
400 Market Street, Suite 400
Philadelphia, PA 19106, USA

www.jkp.com

Library of Congress Cataloging in Publication Data
Reynolds, Kate E.
Sexuality and severe autism : a practical guide for parents,
caregivers and health educators / Kate E.
Reynolds.
pages cm
Includes bibliographical references and index.
ISBN 978-1-84905-327-3 (alk. paper)
1. Sex--Handbooks, manuals, etc. 2. Autism spectrum
disorders--Handbooks, manuals, etc. I. Title.
HQ23.R496 2014
618.92'85882--dc23
2013029391

British Library Cataloguing in Publication Data
A CIP catalogue record for this book is available from the British Library

ISBN 978 1 84905 327 3
eISBN 978 0 85700 666 0

Printed and bound in Great Britain by Bell & Bain Ltd, Glasgow

Here it is;
if only you were.

For my niece,
Amy Alexandra Reynolds,
24 February 1986 – 19 January 2013

With love and thanks to her parents, Marion and Graeme,
for shaping Amy into such a lovely young woman.

Acknowledgements

Many thanks to Jill Owen, head teacher, Chris Smith, ASD Coordinator, and Jodie Watts, Behaviour Analyst, of St Nicholas School, Chippenham, for sharing their knowledge and experiences.

Also thanks to Ingrid Lancaster-Gaye, head teacher, and Sarah Devine, PSHE Coordinator, at Rowdeford School, Rowdeford, Wiltshire. Sarah's input was invaluable.

Thanks to Sue Hatton and Fiona Speirs for their insights, experiences and time.

If only the world were full of David Stewarts! Thanks to the head teacher of Oak Field School in Nottingham.

The JKP team deserve a mention, particularly Maya Barahona, who suffered my video gaffes, and Lucy Buckroyd, who answered whatever inane questions I asked.

With thanks to the following members of staff at The Manor School in Melksham, which my son attends: class teachers Kerry Wootton and Emma Shires; teaching assistants Carolyn Britten, Amanda Fordham, Jo Holdway, Debbie Lanc, Aaron McCaldon, Linda Mence, Aileen Rich and Marie Vincent.

I also wish to thank Rachel Crowder, whose happy demeanour and warmth make her a pleasure to be around.

Many thanks to Bridget Collins, teacher, Emma Howe, student support, and Joy Whitehead, school matron, who have supported my daughter so well in Sheldon School, Chippenham.

Also love to my parents, Sandra and Peter Reynolds, who lost their first grandchild in Amy.

Finally, nothing's complete without my two children, Francesca and Jude.

Contents

Preface

My ten-year-old son is a source of constant worry to me. Having been diagnosed as having severe end autism disorder (classic/childhood autism), he has progressed to what might be termed 'moderate' autism with a continuing severe speech delay. However, his social awareness, ability to locate and communicate feelings, and his functioning in the social world, all still show huge deficits.

As I'll outline in this book, our autistic children (and others with learning difficulties) feature disproportionately highly in figures for being the subject of sexual abuse and being abusers. The former is largely because we traditionally cosset such youngsters, believing misguidedly that we are protecting them, whereas we are leaving them vulnerable. The latter hinges on teaching our children through explicit methods and modelling the basic rules around growing up, appropriate public and private behaviours, sense of self and sense of others, appropriate touch and other factors.

We never know how much our children will develop in the long term. Autistic children hanker for routine and learn at this early stage routines that may be difficult or impossible to shift in older years. What we do today will affect their chances of developing more tomorrow. This book is for those with severely autistic young children, seeking guidance about sexuality, when to introduce the subject, what to say and how to say it. It is also for the many parents whose children are now adults and who are experiencing specific difficulties with their behaviours.

Being an autism parent can be isolating and depressing. It affects our social and family contacts and can leave us feeling imprisoned in our own homes because of our children's behaviours. We can feel constantly under attack for how we manage our children, especially in public. Our society does not readily accept difference, particularly in the case of sexual behaviours. This book will give you proactive strategies to tackle your child's behaviours.

Most information and research I use is based on people with learning disabilities or difficulties (debate continues about which of these is a more appropriate term). There is little literature about the severe end of the autism spectrum specifically and scant information for parents about sexuality and severe autism.

Every family is different in terms of belief systems, cultural, religious and other factors. Parenting styles and personalities also differ and directly affect a child's upbringing. Family situation, such as sole/single parenthood and whether or not there are siblings, will have a bearing on parental choices and decisions. All these influences create a complex set of issues within any family. This book cannot give answers to every family's needs. What I seek to do is to give a broad hearing to the dominant issues surrounding sexuality and severe autism and offer strategies and practical advice to address these.

During the course of researching this book, I have met some teaching professionals with unambiguous awareness that sexuality is a key concept to convey to our autistic children. Unfortunately, they do not appear to be the majority and I believe that education needs wholesale rethinking of how it approaches this subject and prioritises it. As things stand, our severely autistic children can leave school with a minimum of sex education. This should be radically altered for society's well-being as well as that of the individual. From unwanted pregnancies to creating sexual vulnerability and unwitting sexual offenders, we need to address this issue.

Sexual identity, sexual health and sexuality are fundamental to all human beings, regardless of disability or difficulty. However, as parents or caregivers of severely autistic children, we are too often left without relevant information, access and support to know the how, when and what of educating our children about sex. In 2011, I attended a sexuality workshop for parents and caregivers and was astounded that the work we did was almost exactly that which

I would have facilitated with generic groups in the mid-1990s when I worked in HIV/AIDS. It was so non-specific to the needs of the group that many basic questions went unanswered. When autism parents attend this kind of workshop, they are seeking help because, for example, their child masturbates in public. They don't care at this point whether or not genital mutilation is a common practice in other countries, which was one of the areas answered in the sexuality session. They come for practical answers to common problems which they cannot discuss with any other 'experts' because there often aren't any 'experts' in their world. If their child is smearing faeces, they need to understand that they are not alone in this and there are ways of tackling it, which will improve or remove the behaviour.

To clarify the terminology in this book, I mainly use 'severe autism' to depict the profound behaviours of people at the extreme end of the autism spectrum. Having discussed possible language with autism parents, most understood clearly a notion of severe or severe end autism. The term 'intellectual disabilities' tends to be used in papers from Australia and 'learning disabilities' is used widely in the UK. I occasionally use one or other of these phrases when a broader term is needed or when research which refers solely to severe end autism is not available. I refer to 'non-spectrum' people or 'mainstream' schools, meaning that the individuals involved are not on the autism spectrum. I discuss 'children' from the perspective of parenting, so they may be young or adult offspring, which will be patent from the context.

I refer to 'autism mothers/fathers/parents', meaning they have children on the autism spectrum. 'Caregivers' implies all those who give paid care to a person who has severe autism. 'Health educators' are any people who support learning about health issues, including teachers, social care staff, occupational therapists and other allied medical workers and parents. Although this book addresses parents, it is highly relevant to all health educators who work with people with severe autism and gives insight into the challenges all autism parents face on a daily basis. The practical strategies given can be used in or adapted for different settings. Chapter 7 examines some of the difficulties faced by educational and social care establishments, offering parents some idea of the perspective of these paid staff. The overall hope is that parents and other health educators will unite to provide consistent sexuality support for those on the severe end of the autism spectrum.

CHAPTER 1

THE CONTEXT OF SEXUALITY AND SEVERE AUTISM

This chapter sets the scene for the entire book. Attitudes and belief systems constitute the environment within which severely autistic children exist and have immense bearing on whether or not they thrive socially and sexually. Here, I outline definitions of sexuality and severe autism as they are used throughout the text, accepting that these children will vary widely in functioning. The social context of these children's lives directly influences their ability to exercise sexual rights. Parents' values and beliefs have a huge impact on their children, so I pick through some of the key factors which explain the social boundaries placed on severely autistic children. In briefly examining the history of learning difficulties, it is clear that significant progress has been made to emancipate such children, yet they continue to struggle to have a voice in terms of sexuality.

WHAT IS SEXUALITY?
Sexuality is a broad and complex concept, with definitions encompassing anything from sexual acts, gender roles, expression of sexual feelings and fantasies to same-sex relationships. All facets of sexuality are influenced by society and its structures.

Although acknowledging that the following dimensions of sexuality may not be experienced or acted on, the World Health Organization (WHO 2004) describes sexuality as:

- being integral to all human beings throughout life

- incorporating sex, gender identities, gender roles, sexual orientation, eroticism, pleasure, intimacy and reproduction

- being experienced and expressed in thoughts, fantasies, desires, beliefs, attitudes, values, behaviour, practices, roles and relationships

- being influenced by the interaction of biological, psychological, social, economic, political, cultural, ethical, legal, historical, religious and spiritual factors.

Tissot (2009) narrows the term to 'individual sexuality' and instead uses the phrase 'sexual identity', meaning individuals':

- sexual orientation: their 'fantasies, attachments and longings', which may or may not be acted on in reality (Laumann 1994; Reiter 1989)

- sexual preferences: those to whom they are sexually attracted

- gender roles: the social and behavioural norms in a given society

- individual sexuality: how people perceive and express themselves as being sexual.

Similarly complex is the process of sexual development, for which social skills and communication are critically important.

For some parents and caregivers, 'sexuality' may seem an inappropriate term to apply to people with severe autism, but Gerhardt (2006) would counter that:

> sexuality, at its core, is simply part of being human. As such, the avoidance of any discussion of sexuality and/or sexuality instruction as it pertains to learners with ASD constitutes, in effect, a tacit denial of their humanity, which is unacceptable. (Gerhardt 2006, p.1)

Tissot (2009) identifies the following key factors which impact on how adolescents develop individual sexual identity:

- societal attitudes
- where the individual is on the autism spectrum and whether or not there is an underlying learning disability
- the belief system of parents or primary caregivers
- the individual's belief system
- restrictions on teaching about private activities.

Sexual health requires a positive and respectful approach to sexuality and sexual relationships, as well as the possibility of having pleasurable and safe sexual experiences, free of coercion, discrimination and violence.

WHAT IS SEVERE AUTISM?

Autism spectrum disorder (ASD) covers a range of lifelong neurological conditions, medically diagnosed according to observed and reported behaviours, which are categorised in the *International Classification of Diseases* (WHO 1992) and the United States' *Diagnostic and Statistical Manual* (American Psychiatric Association 2000). As yet, there are no scientifically validated physical or genetic tests which are commercially available for use in diagnosis. ASDs are characterised by deficits in social communication (such as speech delay), social interaction (such as following their own 'agenda' of activities) and social imagination (such as prolonged repetitive behaviours) (see Appendix 1).

Diagnosis may incorporate the Childhood Autism Rating Scale (CARS), an assessment tool which attributes scores to a child according to a series of criteria (Schopler, Reicher and Renner 1986). The resulting score on the scale indicates if the child is mildly to severely autistic and differentiates between autism and other developmental delays. Sometimes autistic children may be attributed a 'mental age' which lay people readily understand but can be unhelpful in autism, where some aspects of a child's development may be profoundly delayed, while others in that same child are advanced. The concept of 'mental age' can also fix in parents' and workers' minds that the person concerned is 'stuck' at that age and may contribute to them being treated persistently as a very young, dependent child, thus closing the door to accepting that person may continue to develop and be sexual.

Research suggests that 1 in 100 children in the UK is on the autism spectrum (Baird *et al.* 2006) and 1 in 88 in the United States (Centers for Disease Control and Prevention 2012). About 70 per cent of people with ASDs have learning disabilities and nearly half have an intelligence quotient (IQ) of less than 50 (American Psychiatric Association 2000).

In practice this means that in the UK seven out of ten autistic children have additional learning disabilities, while about one in every five has an IQ below 50 (the average IQ being 85–114). I would argue that in many cases, it is difficult to assess either condition due to individuals' inability to engage in assessment tools and approaches. It is, of course, this profound difficulty in social communication that defines them as severely autistic.

Autism spectrum disorder is an umbrella term which covers the following conditions:

- autism disorder/classic autism/childhood autism/typical autism*

- Asperger syndrome

- Rett syndrome*

- childhood disintegrative disorder (CDD)*

- pervasive developmental disorder not otherwise specified (PDD-NOS), including atypical autism (where symptoms do not fit wholly into an autism disorder diagnosis).

The asterisk (*) denotes a condition more associated with lower defined intelligence and learning disabilities. It is these more severely autistic people that this book addresses.

THEORY OF MIND

Theory of Mind was first mooted by Premack and Woodruff (1978). It proposes that humans have the ability to understand other people's state of mind, such as their wants and thoughts, in a way that allows us to possibly predict what others are likely to do. Some people are more able to apply theory of mind, while others with developmental or cognitive dysfunction have pronounced lesser ability. Empathy is part of this theory and is related to emotions (Premack and Woodruff 1978).

In autism spectrum disorder, theory of mind is challenged, so individuals have difficulty engaging in meaningful social communication, which involves understanding how others might think or feel and acting on that. Severely autistic children lack social imagination; they cannot perceive how others might feel or react and project what might happen based on previous experience (Wing 1981). They often behave in ritualistic patterns or impulsively. Sexuality is largely an emotional experience for the self and others, which develops through social communication and interaction. During social exchanges, such as conversation, individuals learn the rules of society and what are appropriate behaviours. The essence of sexuality is that it is shaped through a process of practice, experimentation and experience whether alone or with others.

If we apply theory of mind to sexuality, we can see that autistic people have considerable challenges to developing as sexual beings. Often they cannot engage effectively in social experiences, partly due to the nature of autism. The other critical reasons for their lack of sexual development are social attitudes to what are perceived as disabled people being sexual. In addition, parental attitudes directly affect opportunities for autistic people to engage effectively in relationships. I explore all these points below.

THE CONTEXT
Parental Grieving

One of the least examined areas of research into autism is that of grieving. Without doubt, parents of either gender grieve when they hear that their child has autism. This is for loss of hopes and projections they had for their child, based on their outlook on life and personal experiences. Most rites of passage – career, marriage, parenthood – may not happen for their child and the impact of this knowledge can be devastating. Every parent inherently wants their child to be a 'mini-him/her' depending on the child's gender.

A long-term, neurological condition, such as autism, shatters this perception.

More than this, the diagnosis will fundamentally alter their roles as parents. Thoughts about childrearing involve a cycle of rearing, letting go so that children can create their own lives, participating as grandparents, then being supported by adult children when ageing or facing illness. Patterns of life that do not conform to this scenario necessitate mourning because our expectations and hopes have been undermined or destroyed without choice. Parents' future lives will be altered in ways they hadn't anticipated and haven't chosen. This lack of choice breeds a feeling of helplessness because they feel out of control. It is interesting that one of the characteristics of autism is a resistance to change and this is clear when a child's routine is altered without what they consider to be due warning; the child responds with challenging behaviours and labile emotions. Yet non-spectrum adults and children do not like change thrust upon them, especially not permanent change, without their input or choice.

Their child's diagnosis introduces stressors to the parents' relationship that were not there before and can exacerbate pre-existing relationship difficulties. Research has shown that marriages of autism parents do not dissolve at any higher rate than those of parents with non-spectrum children in the early years following diagnosis. For non-spectrum families, the dependence of children lessens after eight years of age, reducing the strains between parents who can rebuild or reignite the relationship that pre-existed their children. This is part of an accepted pattern that parents inwardly acknowledge, even if it is difficult to adapt to at the time within a marriage or union. For parents of severely autistic children, the challenge is far greater. Their future will continue to be affected by the dependence of children with all the stress and distress that causes within their relationship. It is this long-term situation that causes marriages of autism parents to break down. Research demonstrates that the rate of divorce in non-spectrum marriages decreases after the youngest child reaches the age of eight, whereas the rate continues at the same level for autism marriages. In effect this means that the totality of divorces is greater and is 60 per cent higher than the average rate of divorce when there are autistic children in the family (Ambitious About Autism (AAA) 2013).

Kübler-Ross (1969) first examined grieving as a process in relation to terminal illness. She categorised the emotions involved into stages which, although not linear in pattern, most patients moved through to the point of eventually accepting their own diagnosis of cancer (Kübler-Ross 1969). This staging has been used in a very practical way in grief counselling, to enable those 'left behind' to manage the emotions around death and move forward to a point where they don't forget the loved one, but they can engage in living again. Since Kübler-Ross's early work, mourning has been re-examined and applied to other areas of life, such as divorce, redundancy and loss of parents. Occasionally, clients in grief counselling may become stuck at one stage of grieving and it is one role of the counsellor to enable the client to move through the process of grieving.

I would argue that grieving is apparent in parents when their child is given a medical diagnosis which has permanent, life-changing impact on the child's socially expected pattern of future life. As a former HIV/AIDS counsellor, it is inconceivable that an HIV positive diagnosis would have been given without offering a comprehensive package of support for the individual, including ongoing counselling and regular specialist input. In the UK it appears to be accepted practice to give parents a diagnosis of autism for their child with little emotional support, save recommending that the parents scour the internet or contact the National Autistic Society (NAS) or similar.

Many autistic children have limited medical follow-up, which is largely to prescribe medication, without reference to the wider issues using a multidisciplinary team. Emotional support seems to be the remit of mental health teams of psychiatrists and therapists, whose intervention may be sought only when there is a crisis, for example when the child's behaviours become difficult to manage or when the family is under severe strain. At this point, it is likely that the child and surrounding family have had considerable negative experiences and formed patterns of working that may be entrenched and hard to shift, even with expert mental health input. For support to be effective, it needs to be proactive, before severe strains are felt within the family which is, after all, providing the most fundamental and basic support for the child.

Although the Autism Act 2009 in the UK recommends local autism teams, these have yet to materialise and will be subject to local design, constrained by local resources. Autism websites are straining with concerns of parents, many of which would be alleviated by effective support from outside the family. I include in this educational establishments (preschools, schools), medical input (health visitor, family doctor, ASD consultant) and other therapists (occupational therapists, speech and language therapists, social workers). These are, of course, paid support staff. Support from unpaid members of the wider society or extended family also can be constructive, although their responses are hugely variable.

In the absence of immediate and ongoing emotional support to facilitate the grieving process, many parents will mourn the perceived 'loss' of their child for prolonged periods. There are often signs of continuing grieving years after diagnosis. As a trained counsellor, I would argue that many autism parents are 'stuck' in the grieving process, usually at the stage of anger or depression. Yet parents are expected to participate in decision-making about their children's futures when they are grieving and without emotional support. These decisions are important, especially in children's early years when all evidence points to life chances being vastly improved with effective educational and therapeutic input at this point.

Guilt

Perhaps one of the most unspoken emotions associated with having conceived a disabled child is guilt. Parents may experience a sense of responsibility or even regret for having brought such a child into the world, which often is perceived as dangerous even for non-spectrum children. Such a perception is highlighted by increasingly controlled play environments and fears associated with letting non-spectrum children play outdoors or without close supervision.

Parents try to protect their children from what they perceive as dangers in society, such as bullying, exploitation or sometimes even the blows of the realities of life like redundancy or the end of relationships. Some parents are better than others at allowing their offspring to experience difficulties in order to grow and develop strategies to manage future negative experiences. Others are more controlling over the lives of their children, which can prevent their children maturing emotionally and becoming independent beings. Wherever people are on the continuum of parenting, their responses can be sharpened when they discover their child has autism, especially at the more severe end.

Being the parent of a child who is perceived as and labelled as 'disabled' brings with it a range of new societal and personal expectations. As individuals, it may heighten parents' desires to protect their children, especially when cases of violence towards less able autistic children are highlighted in the media. Guilt is often a deep-seated response by parents to realising that they have 'afflicted' this world on their less-than-able child. In most cases of autism disorder, the child's life expectancy will not be lessened by the condition per se so parents have to confront the fact that their child will probably outlive them. For some parents, this may act as a stimulus to ensure the child is as independent as possible and has a stable network of support for when they (the parents) are no longer alive or capable of overseeing certain aspects of their child's life. For others, the knowledge that their child will need ongoing support from other people in what is perceived as an unfriendly and uncaring world may compound their guilt and cause chronic anxiety about future provision for their child.

Social judgements about conceiving a 'disabled' child can also impact on personal feelings of guilt. As a genetic condition, albeit with other factors involved, autism often affects more than one child in a family and parents can feel judged about conceiving more than one disabled child – as if they should have 'learned' after the first one. In practice, autism tends to be diagnosed around two to three years of age, even later for higher functioning autism, so parents frequently already have more than one child when the first diagnosis is made.

Parents also may feel guilt towards other siblings whom they feel unable to give the necessary time and attention to because the autistic child is soaking up their personal resources

(Henderson 2012). Siblings may be unable to live a 'normal' family life. They may feel unable to bring friends home to play because of the autistic child; family days out may routinely involve only one parent because the other has to care for the autistic sibling. Additionally, siblings may be left with the responsibility of severely autistic brothers or sisters, which will impact significantly on their futures and can be a source of guilt and distress to parents. In the UK, there is some support given through Young Carers for siblings (see Resources).

I would argue that autism parents sometimes demonstrate feelings of guilt by looking outwards, trying to find factors which caused their child's autism and over which they have no control. As research stands, ASDs are multifactorial in cause, although genes from probably both parents are underlying all cases. Many parents might dispute that genetics are involved in causation; science disproves this. The genetic link has the potential to nail guilt to parents unless they can work through the emotion, which is most constructively achieved through counselling.

Parental Belief Systems

The family environment is usually dominated by parents' belief systems and is the site of children's adolescent development. Autistic or not, offspring absorb personal boundaries, relationships and social norms they experience within the family. If they exist in an environment where boundaries are weak or unclear, or with violence or sexual abuse, children may develop warped perceptions of sexuality.

Regardless of whether or not a child has autism and where they are on the spectrum, the information they receive directly from their parents will be coloured by their parents' own experiences and knowledge. Certainly, religious and cultural beliefs have a strong influence on what support parents give to the development of their child's sexual identity (Kaeser 1996; Murphy and Young 2005). This may be particularly true of homosexuality, which remains a taboo in many cultures, yet there is no reason to suppose its prevalence is any less in those with severe communication difficulties than it is in other populations. Research in Ireland has found that most caregivers felt that people with learning disabilities had a right to relationships but only 42 per cent agreed that homosexuality between consenting partners was acceptable (Family Planning Association (FPA) and Public Health Agency 2010).

Despite a societal increase in information available about sexual health since the 1960s, many parents do not feel equipped to discuss sex with their offspring. Non-spectrum children may not want to discuss the subject with parents, preferring to glean knowledge from peers. However, children who have autism, especially those regarded as more severely affected, do not have the capacity to learn through 'osmosis' from peers, partly because their peers will probably have similar conditions. Osmosis is taken to mean by observation or subtle social clues such as body language, which are clear deficits in severe autism. Instead, they need explicit and detailed guidance about everything from naming body parts and understanding their function in sex, through the processes involved in sex, possible outcomes of having sex, negative experiences and how to recognise and report abuse. This list can seem overwhelming to parents, particularly if they are not adequately equipped with either knowledge or confidence to manage such issues. Unease about broaching sexuality can be worsened if autistic children become aroused when being assisted to wash or dress, leading to embarrassment for parents or caregivers.

Due to the perceived level of their disability, such children often do not have the opportunities to socialise independently of their parents or caregivers. Even in social situations, autistic children at the severe end of the spectrum tend to be stripped of chances to develop socially, such as being encouraged and expected to ask for a drink at a social gathering, or being left with other children while parents and caregivers watch from a distance. In my experience, this happens increasingly as autistic children become young adults and parents appear to close their minds to the possibility that their children might continue to develop socially and cognitively. By this stage many parents are worn down by poor experiences in public or simply have become accustomed to taking over for their child in a 'does he take sugar' manner.

Sometimes parents rely on older siblings to give information to severely autistic children. This approach can be fraught with difficulty. I met one sole (single) mother who depended on her older son to tell her younger lower functioning autistic son about sexual health. She did so, because she felt wholly inadequate to address the subject: she had received no informal instruction from her own mother and she had very limited sexual experience of men. However, she had no idea what information her older child was giving the younger son, how that information was being processed and whether or not it was understood. Her stated feeling was that she hoped the school or 'someone else' would take up the reins and inform her child in her absence.

Studies have found that parents felt as if they were left with the responsibility of teaching their children about how to tackle the subject of sexuality. For the more forthright parents, it was felt to be similar to other information or services, which have to be fought for by whatever means available (Garbutt 2008). If they have no active support and education, profoundly autistic children and young adults ultimately may glean information from the media, using television dramas or movies to learn about relationships. They may also locate pornography sites on the internet. The difficulty with any of these sources is that the autistic person cannot check how accurate the information is, or discuss how any of the characters might be feeling in order to gauge if the behaviours they are witnessing are positive, negative or even appropriate (Garbutt 2008; McCabe 1999). These children may develop a distorted sense of power in relationships, derived from watching soap operas, for example, which are full of dramatic and often aggressive incidents.

One of the biggest concerns for parents of severely autistic females is pregnancy. Whereas historically women with learning or intellectual disabilities were given enforced sterilisation procedures, their reproductive rights are protected in many western countries today. In reality, there are many options for contraception which negate any need for sterilisation to prevent pregnancy and do not rely on the woman's memory or cognitive abilities, such as injections of contraceptives. What many parents should understand is that sterilisation does not reduce sexual desire or libido.

Sole (Single) Parents

Most sole autism parents are women, largely due to divorce and the propensity to give mothers residential custody of any children resulting from the marriage; this is replicated in civil partnerships. Ironically, most children with ASDs will be male. There is a ratio of four to one males to females in autism disorder (classic/childhood autism) and other more severe forms of autism. This is aside from Rett syndrome, which affects only females in adulthood, due to infant death of boys affected.

Ultimately, sole parents deal with cross-gender caring issues and no area presents with greater challenges than sexuality. If the child's father is alive and there are no issues of violence, I would always tell sole mothers to ensure that fathers are involved with childrearing, regardless of any personal issue between divorced parents. I would advise the same for fathers who have residential custody of children. Same-gender role models are incredibly important in the social development of all children, affording them insight into essential 'maleness' for boys and 'femaleness' for girls. Men and women operate differently in the social world and educate their children by their actions and behaviours. Fathers or male caregivers tend to be more relaxed and activity focused, whereas mothers or female caregivers are often more nurturing and controlled, so children also have different experiences with each parent (Wilson *et al.* 2009). Although severely autistic children tend not to learn by osmosis, in the long term, they appear to learn from repeatedly watching role models, especially those in the home.

Certain caregiving behaviours can be more pronounced or prolonged due to being in a sole parent household. For example, in my experience of autism mothers, allowing a child of either gender to remain sleeping in the mother's bed for years beyond that which might be 'acceptable' in non-spectrum children is relatively common. The likelihood of this happening is lessened in marriages, where the adult male is also in the bed. When this does occur it causes immense strain to the adult relationship, since the male usually capitulates and sleeps in a different bed. Although this may feel to the mother like a caring act, it can serve the purpose of lessening intimacy with the male partner, perhaps because the mother is exhausted or she simply doesn't want sexual relations but needs the father for other reasons, such as financial, physical, moral or emotional support.

An extensive period when a child may sleep in the mother's bed is potentially extremely damaging for the child. Autistic children like routine and have an almost pathological fear of change, which they will resist strenuously. This means such children will have entrenched perceptions that sleeping with adults is 'OK'. Not only will this be tough to alter, but also such children will be more vulnerable to sexual abuse from other adults, since there won't be a concept that sleeping with one adult is 'OK' and with another it is not. So this initially caring act can create the foundations for future sexual abuse.

Another key area to develop skills is in toileting. Sole mothers of boys may have difficulty with this. One of the most helpful aspects of fathering boys is in teaching by example how to use the lavatory by standing and the social norms of using men's public lavatories. Mothers of boys tend to take them into the women's lavatories, often sharing a cubicle. This is especially true when the child has profound communication difficulties. Parents may use lavatories for disabled people, but sometimes these will not be in working order or simply do not exist in some places. It is critical for boys' and girls' future safety and well-being that they learn to use public lavatories independently and do not get into the habit of being routinely observed in the lavatories, leaving clear possibilities for sexual abuse.

Cross-Gender Caring

For many autistic people, learning is a long process, often involving repetition of basic information before this can be built on with more complex issues. The same is true of sexual education.

The prolonged level of dependence in autism impacts on fathers, who may have to help with caring tasks for their daughters in adulthood, after a mother has become incapacitated or has died. In addition, divorce rates ensure that fathers may have to engage in intimate tasks for their daughters when they have them for weekends, for example. Of course, either scenario (mothers helping sons and fathers helping daughters) can happen within a marriage or union.

It may be difficult for a mother to talk with full knowledge about certain aspects of male sexuality, such as wet dreams or erections, when she cannot experience them or she is simply too embarrassed. Fathers may find discussing menstruation (periods) with their daughters problematical because they will never have experienced them, or may feel unqualified and uncomfortable. Although fathers and mothers may have had some sexual health conversations with their own parents, it may not have incorporated issues about the opposite gender, so their information base may be low and they may have been socialised not to openly discuss sexual issues.

It may be tempting to use films or television programmes about physical changes or childbirth to 'educate' our children, but without sufficient preparation and support this can be frightening. Consequences of such anxiety can be self-injurious behaviours.

Protection

Legislation and social policy around disability have promoted individual rights and access to or involvement in creating services, leaving issues of sexuality and relationships less of a priority. Similarly, in education, where the trend has been to 'normalise' the roles of those with learning difficulties (Garbutt 2008; Wolfensberger 1972), this is not happening in relation to sexuality and relationships (Garbutt 2008; Shakespeare, Gillespie-Sells and Davies 1996). Instead, intimate relationships tend to be seen in terms of risk reduction and social danger with parents having the least positive responses to sexuality and relationships.

Research is needed to confirm this, but it seems a reasonable assumption that parents of more severely autistic children are similar to those parents of offspring with learning difficulties in terms of feeling the impulse to protect them, more so than mainstream children. Hollomotz (2011) describes such overprotection as:

> parental protection that is disproportionate, taking into account the developmental level and abilities of the child. It is characterised by excessive physical and social contact, prolonged infantilisation, active prevention of independent behaviour and social maturity and excessive parental control. (Hollomotz 2011, p.44)

Overprotection may be partly derived from a misplaced, internalised feeling that protecting an autistic child from dangers (real and imagined) alleviates the pain of guilt. It is a way of compensating for inflicting autism on our children. Overprotection in itself leaves severely autistic children more open to abuse, because children don't gain experiences of life and opportunities for education which would equip them against potential abusers (Hollomotz 2011).

The 'sick role' was identified by Talcott Parsons, a sociologist, who proposed that people adopt this social role when they are physically unwell (Parsons 1951). Part of the theory is that sick people are regarded as legitimately unemployed or fulfilling other social roles due to illness, over which they have no control. In turn, they are expected to behave in particular ways; to seek medical help, conform to all medical treatment or advice and be seen to be trying to get well.

A similar functional theory can be applied to parents moulding into a 'carer's/caregiver's role', this being socially constructed. The primary caregiver is permitted not to engage in the paid workforce due to the demands of a disabled other. Certain state financial benefits legitimise this, such as Carer's Allowance in the UK. They can also avoid specific rules for the rest of society, such as queuing, using main entrances to buildings or paying full price in some circumstances. The caregiver's obligation to society might incorporate seeking and using all medical, educational and other support for their disabled child and ensuring others are aware of the disability. Marshall, Anderson and Fernandez (1999) found that sometimes parents and health staff unwittingly collude in this:

> Therapists can unintentionally obtain information that fits preconceived beliefs and patients can report information that conforms to expectations that may be unstated – expectations of a treatment culture. (Marshall *et al.* 1999, p.53)

The caregiver's role might entail being overprotective of (in this case) their autistic children, being apologetic for their offspring's disability and any disturbance this might cause to others, and avoiding using mainstream facilities when those for disabled people are available.

Some parents gain recognition that they haven't experienced before through having the label of 'carer/caregiver'; the harder the job, the greater the appreciation of their role by others. Paradoxically, this can encourage promotion of dependence in their autistic children and reduce (if subconsciously) parents' attempts to develop opportunities for their children to reach as independent as possible a life. Interestingly, on the issue of children sleeping with their parents, I've heard many excuses from 'he's only comfortable in our bed' to 'he had a meltdown, so I gave in'. By permitting this behaviour, parents are in effect promoting dependence and the very behaviour that will lay their offspring open to abuse. It is true that sleep disturbances are common in early years autism and at other points during the lifespan, such as when autistic people are unwell or in unfamiliar surroundings. However, parents tend to portray sleep issues as intractable symptoms of autism that they can do nothing constructive about, so they seek reassurance to this effect from other autism parents and often get it if they approach autism support websites.

The irony of the existence of overprotection is that in practice, it undermines the opportunities for an autistic child to have experiences and develop skills which allow them to be socially independent. Without the chance to walk to the local postbox or pay for a cake at the coffee shop, for example, children grow into adults whose role becomes socially constructed to be dependent on a caregiver or parent. Hollomotz (2011) builds a broad case that overprotection from risk actually can increase the vulnerability of children to sexual abuse, which is predominantly perpetrated by someone in children's inner circle of social contacts (Hollomotz 2011).

Overprotection limits social contacts beyond a tight inner circle and controls experiences so that children may not be aware of what constitutes acceptable and unacceptable behaviours. In turn, they are less able to protect themselves due to lack of independent thought and action and knowledge of where to seek help or services. Even being able to wash and dress independently is a critical part of this. In harbouring dependence, overprotection can leave a child more vulnerable because of the nature of the relationships which can involve intimate caring tasks, with the child having a strictly limited circle of social contacts.

Children as Sexual Beings

Non-spectrum children engage in sexualised behaviours, but these may seem more pronounced in children with autism because the age at which they reach developmental stages may be delayed. For example, it is fairly common for preschool children to explore and stimulate their own bodies, sometimes in public (Cavanagh Johnson 1999). Children and adolescents with autism may also engage in these behaviours but in adolescence or adulthood when it is perceived as sexually provocative and unacceptable.

Even in non-spectrum parent–child relations, parents can experience difficulty perceiving their offspring as sexual (and vice versa). This feeling is emphasised when a child has severe autism. Studies show that parental attitudes can be instrumental in moderating their children's experiences or access to possibilities of intimate relationships (Johnson *et al.* 2002; Szollos and McCabe 1995).

Often, parents are concerned that educating their severely autistic children about sexual health and relationships will encourage sexual behaviours or interest, so only permit schools to support this learning when their child is already showing signs of sexuality, such as masturbation (Tissot 2009). They are also keen to have liaison with schools about any sex education their child receives and have views about behaviours they feel are acceptable, such as hand-holding and kissing, but want staff to actively discourage masturbation (FPA and Public Health Agency 2010). Almost all sexualised behaviours appear to be regarded by many parents as 'behaviours of concern', although these are specifically defined as follows:

> Culturally abnormal behaviours, of such an intensity, frequency or duration that the physical safety of the person or others is likely to be placed in serious jeopardy, or behaviour which is likely to seriously limit the use of, or result in the person being denied access to ordinary community facilities. (Emerson 2001, p.3, quoted in McVilly 2007, p.7)

Inappropriate sexual behaviour in severely autistic children is not usually that. It is sexually appropriate behaviour acted upon in an inappropriate situation or place. This usually occurs because the individual has not been sexually educated at all, sufficiently or effectively. However, this is not an excuse under the law and children can be arrested for such behaviours as masturbating or exposing their genitalia in a public place. This is one critical area that parents of children at the more extreme end of the autism spectrum should comprehend; if children do not learn about sexual relationships, this creates greater potential for them to behave illegally as they mature into adults when they will be held responsible for their actions. The judiciary may show leniency due to a severe autism diagnosis but such children could effectively be incarcerated in a social care institution or monitored continuously as a result of their inappropriate behaviours.

Lack of communication skills in autism can promote the idea that individuals cannot adequately understand sexual as well as social situations, rendering them 'vulnerable'. Furthermore, the impulse to protect children from danger is magnified in sexual issues, when people are at their most intimate and exposed and when abuse is known to happen with lasting, destructive implications.

Even when parents accept the need for our adolescent children to experiment with relationships, they have concerns about social judgements of their children and a lack of knowledge as to how much our children truly understand about sexual issues. Yet it is possible to educate severely autistic children to understand relationships, appropriate behaviours and social rules, regardless of communication issues. It takes understanding, courage and the strategies identified in later chapters.

Social Pressures

Historically, society has viewed intellectually disabled people as having two conflicting ways of being perceived sexually. They are regarded either as 'asexual' and infantile or 'childlike' (Kaeser 1996; Murphy and Young 2005) or as a group which is potentially dangerous to their non-disabled counterparts (Scott, Jackson and Backett-Milburn 1998).

In western society, there are expectations about what is 'polite' and this may include some actions that are not perceived as intimate, but may be confusing for children at the severe end of the autism spectrum. For example, giving kisses to relatives and family friends can be difficult for autistic children to discern from kisses between lovers, or they may believe that kissing total strangers as a greeting is appropriate. This is unhelpful for teaching autistic children about acceptable and unacceptable advances from others and opens the door for sexual abuse, in which autistic children may be unaware of appropriate and inappropriate behaviours, unless explicitly taught. This can mean that they act in inappropriate ways, particularly in public.

Many autistic children and adults depend on films or movies, which are easily accessible, for their understanding of behaviour. Although it might be argued that society has progressed, many older movies portray heterosexual relationships in terms of power with a male aggressor and a female as submissive or conquered recipient in sexual terms. I only need think of the scene in *Butch Cassidy and the Sundance Kid* in which Robert Redford's character 'seduces' Katharine Ross's character with a gun, she seeming not to know him as he tells her to 'keep going, teacher lady' as she undresses. This scene involves no nudity, yet the inference of power is palpable. Numerous other movies contain far more explicit and violent scenes of supposed seduction of women by male counterparts.

It is common for autistic children and teens to repeat movies, sometimes playing the same few seconds until they grasp the words or meaning. Social messages about power relations between genders are not wasted on autistic viewers, who may not be able to discern apparent aggression from supposed fantasy foreplay, as depicted in the *Butch Cassidy* scene. The majority being highly visual, autistic movie watchers may extract the perception that men are dominant over women in sexual relations and that aggression, either verbal or physical is acceptable. For autistic males, they may gain a sense that socially correct sexual behaviour involves dominant assertion of sexual 'rights' over women. Equally disturbing is that autistic females receive the message that their sexual role is one of subservience and passivity, leaving them open to unwanted sexual advances and undermining their ability to be assertive in sexual encounters. For most autistic people, life is black and white – there are few grey areas – so laying down foundations of inequality in sexual interactions may be dangerous and entrenched. Much of the content on the internet can give dubious messages about sexual power relations and can be difficult to monitor in severely autistic people, many of whom are very skilled at using computers.

The exponential success of the book *Fifty Shades of Grey* is disturbing (James 2011). From my perspective the story describes how a sexually inexperienced woman is persuaded into a sexually abusive relationship with an older and potentially violent man. The power he wields is clearly far in excess of hers. Yet this has been read and accepted as sexually provocative and even given the credence of 'saving' marriages in the popular press. If a movie is created which is faithful to the book, severely autistic children will be learning a warped and unhealthy perspective of intimate relationships.

Even the law can underpin sexual imbalance and reduce women to a bit-part on a male-oriented stage. Think back to Judge James Pickles' infamous assertion that women who dressed in particular ways invited sexual approaches and were 'asking for it'. Think also of the apparently common misconception that a verbal 'no' actually often means 'yes'.

A Short History of Learning Disabilities

The late nineteenth and early twentieth centuries witnessed a Eugenics movement which dictated that those with learning difficulties had defective genes and should not be permitted to procreate, leading to enforced sterilisation of women and some men (Howard and Hendy 2004). Until the 1990s, when community care policies were introduced in the UK, many people with severe autism and those with learning disabilities lived in institutions, often segregated by gender (Sinson 1995). Within these institutions, sexual relationships were not encouraged (Valios 2002) and individual privacy was rare (Shakespeare *et al.* 1996).

Until fairly recently, sexuality in those with developmental disabilities was ignored and suppressed rather than directly addressed as a credible issue (Watson *et al.* 2002).

In more recent history people with autism and learning difficulties have tended to be viewed as 'eternal children' (McCarthy 1999), that is as asexual and innocent. This fuels the notion that for these people, it can be 'assumed that sexuality was irrelevant because of the young people's level of cognitive and communication impairments' (Morris 2001, p.15). People with learning difficulties have been given the label 'vulnerable' in government policy (Department of Health and Home Office 2000) and thereby considered at risk of being abused, particularly sexually. In turn, this leads to reluctance to encourage intimate relationships for this group of people.

Debate about sexuality and learning difficulties has developed and appears to reinforce the rights of those with milder forms to have sexual identity (Everett 2007). This is also reflected in UK government policy; for example, England's National Curriculum includes personal, social and health education (PSHE), which incorporates sexuality. Yet more profoundly affected autistic children depend on the will of school management to embrace sexuality teaching, which therefore is inconsistent despite the National Curriculum (Department for Children, Schools and Families 2009).

A growing movement of inclusion means that children who would have been in specialist schools in the past are increasingly being taught in mainstream schools. This presents challenges to mainstream teaching, which should engage all students in learning about sexuality but may not have staff with the skills to do so.

In literature related to autism spectrum disorders, there are many books related to higher functioning autism, Asperger syndrome and aspects of sexual identity. However, there is a dearth of information about more severely autistic people; although these individuals' education is also covered by PSHE, this should be differentiated according to their abilities.

Many aspects of teaching sexuality have progressed, but there are many deficits in education and supporting severely autistic adolescents and adults in developing relationships of any kind.

Services and support are variable and appear dependent on belief systems of parents and philosophies of professions.

The Law Relating to Education, Health and Social Services

Social policies and legislation relating to education, health and social services reflect a commitment towards enabling children and young adults to be self-determining and independent and have actively promoted their involvement in shaping services through a process of consultation (Franklin 2008).

In addition, the following legislation in the UK underpins the emancipation of disabled people and their active participation in society:

- The Children Act of 1989 and 2004 aimed to strengthen the children's legal positions, giving their rights and wishes equal weight to parents' and ensuring children were kept informed and consulted.

- The Human Rights Act 1989 states that every human being has a right to respect for private and family life.

- The Disability Discrimination Act 1995 gives people with any kind of impairment, including learning disability, the right to equal treatment in terms of accessing goods and services, which includes services such as family planning clinics and advice centres.

- The Disability Discrimination Act 2005 extended the legal position to cover all aspects of provision by public bodies, not just services, for which the 1995 Act had catered. For example, physical structures, such as entrances to buildings, had to be addressed to embrace disability. In addition, public bodies had to document how they actively promoted equality for disabled people.

- The United Nations Convention on the Rights of the Child 1989 and Convention on the Rights of Persons with Disabilities 2006 reiterate this in a global sense.

This perception of disabled people as wanting and being expected to have an active role in services and autonomy is clear in later policy such as the 2007 document, *Aiming High for Disabled Children: Better Support for Families*, which clearly stated it was the importance of the individual voice of the disabled child, rather than the family's voice, which should be paramount (HM Treasury and Department for Education and Skills 2007). This is an important demarcation to make, because research has shown that families who are integrally involved in planning tend to prioritise issues such as respite, accommodation, day care programmes and therapies, ignoring areas such as relationships and sexuality (Burton-Smith *et al.* 2009). Again in 2007, the Department of Health produced a document relating specifically to transition, *A Transition Guide for All Services: Key Information for Professionals about the Transition Process for Disabled Young People*, followed by a guide for best practice in 2008, *Transition: Moving on Well* (Department of Health and Department for Children, Schools and Families 2007, 2008).

In relation to sexual behaviour and relationships, the Mental Capacity Act 2005 is significant, since it works on an assumption that people have the capacity to be self-determining through decision-making unless it can be proven that a person does not have the mental capacity to do so. It is not sufficient to believe that the person will make an unwise choice; there must be proof that the individual is incapable of taking decisions and only then does another have the right to act in the 'best interest' of the disabled person. This emphasis underpins the rights of people with learning difficulties to make choices within the realm of sexual relationships.

SEXUAL ABUSE

Sexual abuse is not an uncommon event, with around one in six boys and one in four girls suffering before the age of 18 (Centers for Disease Control and Prevention 2013). Those with more profound communication difficulties associated with their ASDs are more than twice as likely as those without disabilities to be affected (Murphy and Young 2005). Some studies have shown figures four times higher for generically disabled children than those without (Sullivan and Knutson 2000).

Children with autism spectrum disorders are susceptible to predatory paedophiles, who can be categorised in the following ways:

- 'easy prey': targeting young, usually female victims

- victim attributes: the child was sexually attractive to the attacker

- opportunity: those who will act opportunistically if a potential offending situation occurs

- circumstance or manipulation: using violence or threat prior to sexual attack.

Children with autism fall into two categories, in that they may be regarded as easy prey and they are open to manipulation or intimidation due to their social challenges, so they may be particularly attractive to sexual abusers (American Psychiatric Association 2000).

Predatory paedophiles have a mind-set that allows them to justify offending and not accepting it as 'wrong' or 'harmful' to the victim. The distortions in their thinking help them to minimise or rationalise their offences towards children (Burn and Brown 2006). They objectify – or view the child as an object – which may be made easier in children whose behaviours, such as stimming, repetitive or stereotyped, are not those that 'ordinary' children would display (Russell 1998).

Research has identified two types of child sexual offenders: groomers and opportunistic sexual abusers (Cavanagh Johnson 1999). First, groomers use pleasant forms of social contact and 'friendship' to 'court' the child and develop a positive relationship with the child, which they mould into a potentially abusive one. During this grooming, the sexual abuser assesses how likely the child is to disclose the abuse. Those children who resist grooming approaches are discarded because of their potential to disclose the behaviour and abuse. Critically, non-verbal autistic children may present as carrying little risk of disclosure, making them more likely to be targeted. Through the child's social deficits and chronic lack of friendships, a paedophile who presents as a 'friend' may be extremely attractive to an autistic child, who may crave and never have experienced this type of relationship before. This makes them less able to recognise manipulation and consequent abuse. It may be even more confusing for a severely autistic child if they are not equipped with knowledge and skill in issues surrounding sexuality and appropriate behaviours. This is fundamentally important in working with an autistic child, because solid self-esteem, knowledge of boundaries of 'right' and 'wrong' in relationships and a broad circle of contacts all increase the child's ability to resist grooming and likelihood to display disclosing behaviours which will deter offenders.

Second, opportunistic sexual abusers use opportunities to target children. Communication and social difficulties associated with autism render this group more susceptible (Cavanagh Johnson 1999). This may be through service provision: Goldman (1994) found that half of victims of sexual abuse were targeted through disability services with which the paedophiles were involved. In this way, it is argued that autistic children in institutions may be at even greater risk of sexual abuse than those who live with their families in the wider community (Goldman 1994).

One of the key principles for parents to understand is that sheltering their intellectually disabled offspring, however profoundly affected they are, actually has the effect of leaving them vulnerable. Children who have little knowledge or experience of relationships, what is appropriate and inappropriate behaviour in a sexual relationship and how to exercise power within an intimate relationship are left wide open to sexual abuse or sexual exploitation. It is the arming of a severely autistic child with information and opportunities to experience relationships and friendships and knowledge of what is, basically, 'right' and 'wrong' in sexual behaviours, which will defend them from abuse, not cosseting them and keeping them hidden from perceived dangers. The irony, of course, is that most sexual abuse is perpetrated by a close family member or someone within the close circle of social contacts around the child. The larger the circle and the more empowered the child, the lesser the risk of sexual abuse happening and the more likely it is to be reported or spotted early.

Residential settings also impact on individual vulnerability to sexual abuse. Whereas some parents might consider that an institution would safeguard their child from what they perceive as a dangerous society, in practice an institution has structures that enhance their vulnerability, such as the following:

- lack of sex education

- segregation: lack of opportunity to socially interact with the opposite gender

- discouragement of opportunities to experience intimate or close friendships

- few chances to take meaningful choices about their lives

- lack of autonomy

- lack of communication with the outside world

- depersonalisation (Hollomotz 2011)

- power relationships with those in authority and their own belief systems and values.

Research in Ireland (FPA and Public Health Agency 2010) found that of 69 adults with learning disabilities, most felt they had limited opportunities to talk about sexual health, even though they wanted to. Furthermore, some staff forbade them from having sexual relationships, although they felt they should be able to determine their own sexual relationships. This happens, despite legislation that patently supports people with intellectual disabilities having sexual relations, if they have capacity to consent. In addition, their understanding of sexual health and surrounding issues was confused and incomplete and had no one to check the accuracy of information.

Of the paid caregivers in the report, most thought that people with learning disabilities had the right to sexual expression. Yet half of these participants did not think that intimate relationships were important to people with learning difficulties. This is an area that needs addressing.

CHAPTER 2

A FRAMEWORK FOR TEACHING SEXUALITY

This chapter addresses the foundations of learning which severely autistic children need to know before they are taught about the mechanics of sex, contraception or sexually transmitted infections. Without developing their core knowledge and skills, these children will not become as competent and confident adults as possible, who are able to deal positively with sexuality and sexual health. The Resources section of the book gives details of many resources to enable parents to do the exercises in this chapter. Basic learning blocks can be developed very early in children's lives and are fundamental to their self-development, personal safety and integration into the community. I regard these as:

- sense of self
- self-esteem
- self-determination
- expressing feelings constructively
- relating to society
- friendships and other relationships.

SEXUAL RIGHTS

For sexual health to be attained and maintained, the sexual rights of all individuals must be respected, protected and fulfilled. Michael and Ann Craft, who worked extensively with people with learning disabilities, cited the following as basic sexual rights (Craft and Craft 1987):

- the right to grow up

- the right to know

- the right to be sexual and to make or break relationships

- the right to be free from the individual sexual attitudes of different caregivers

- the right to be free from abuse

- the right to humane and dignified environments.

Applying this to autistic children, regardless of how profoundly affected they are by autism, we arrive at a pressing need to accept that all human beings are sexual beings and enable these children accordingly. For some parents this will seem morally and culturally unacceptable. For those, I would ask them to understand the alternative to educating and enabling their children to develop sexually:

- A far greater risk of their children being the subject of sexual abuse (Koller 2000).

- An increased risk of their children abusing others (Grieve, McLaren and Lindsay 2006).

- A far greater risk their children will commit sexual offences, such as inappropriate sexual behaviours in public (Stokes and Kaur 2005).

Some parents, I know, will view their children as being too severely autistic to register or engage in any form of sex education. For those, I would say that their children may develop much further than they anticipate. My son was deemed to be 'institution material' when he was first diagnosed with 'classic' autism aged three years.

In fact I was told he would be in residential care within the year and he would be unlikely to speak if he wasn't doing so by seven years of age. Like many parents I absorbed whatever information I could about autism and used available programmes to enable him to develop a relationship with me, followed by relationships with others. Advances in teaching approaches to autism mean that he has developed socially and cognitively in a specialist unit within a mainstream school, which has the advantage of non-spectrum role models. Although his speech remains severely delayed and his social and cognitive skills are extremely limited, I have little doubt he will continue to develop as long as there is input into his life, particularly of a social nature.

Parents need to be guiding their children and ensuring they will manage in life as far as is possible when the parents die. The rules and boundaries they embed in their children's heads as youngsters will carry them into adulthood and beyond. Parents do their children a disservice if they ignore their sexuality and lay them open to abuse or breaching the law.

SEXUAL CYCLE OF SEVERELY AUTISTIC CHILDREN

Young people at the severe end of the autism spectrum will develop physically in similar ways to non-spectrum adolescents, regardless of any intellectual challenges or learning difficulties. Puberty is simply a stage in a cycle of sexual development, which will happen without reference to IQ or social abilities. However, medications and some natural differences in physical maturity may mean that there is a broad variation in the onset of puberty and a subsequent difference in the inception of sexualised behaviours.

Bearing in mind that the impact of hormones in boys can start at ten years old and menstruation in girls can begin at eight years, parents need to start preparing their children from young childhood, not waiting for a clear signal that they are sexual, such as masturbation or the average age of menstruation (12 years) and ejaculation (14 years).

Evidence shows that sex steroid production during puberty creates sexual urges, fantasies and feelings like those of non-spectrum adolescents (Stokes, Newton and Kaur 2007). However, these changes in mood, emotion and sexual desire can be prolonged or delayed (Sullivan and Caterino 2008). Hormones can also be responsible for increases in aggressive behaviour and self-injurious behaviours or emotional outbursts (meltdowns) (Biro and Dorn 2006). Although puberty can mark a regression in some behaviours in around 17 per cent of autistic adolescents, research has shown that at least half those affected will recover and continue to develop (Billstedt, Gillberg and Gillberg 2005).

People with more extreme end ASDs also do not have an inbuilt social barometer which enables them to absorb or acknowledge the response of others and therefore modify their behaviours. Research underpins their inability to recognise subtle social cues or consider others' perspectives (Realmuto and Ruble 1999). If a sexual behaviour feels good, a person with ASD may indulge in it, with a total disregard for others' feelings (Ray, Marks and Bray-Garretson 2004). Specifically, Kalyva (2010) found they had difficulty judging what behaviours were appropriate for public as opposed to private situations. They also had problems attaching any importance to personal hygiene (Kalyva 2010).

Yet work with young people with ASD and learning difficulties demonstrated that they had a desire to understand their autism, how it impacted on others and how they were different from non-spectrum people (Hatton and Tector 2010). So education needs to be explicit about their autism and why this makes them behave in different ways from non-spectrum individuals.

As their children progress through life, parents will need to ensure they are bodily aware, so they notice changes that might indicate pregnancy, sexually transmitted infections or ill-health, and they prepare their daughters for the menopause.

COMMUNICATING SEXUAL INFORMATION

In non-spectrum adolescents, much of their learning is informal via peer groups, leaving the formal teaching about physical changes and the mechanics of sexual behaviour and possible repercussions, such as pregnancy. These latter subjects are adequately incorporated into the UK's National Curriculum (Department for Children, Schools and Families 2009). Severely autistic young people are unlikely to learn from a peer group so the very basic building blocks of sexual knowledge have to be laid by parents or caregivers.

Key Principles of Communicating

Here are some guidelines for parents on the key principles of communicating:

- Start early.

- Don't wait for issues such as masturbation before considering sex as something they should talk about.

- Assume their children are sexual, regardless of communication skills. Research involving mothers has found that the more verbal the child, the more they reported that the child had knowledge of body parts and functions, understood the difference between public and private behaviours, and had received some form of sex education (Ruble and Dalrymple 1993). So it is possible that parents teach less when they get little response from their children. Yet (written) discussions with non-verbal higher functioning autistic people demonstrate that they absorb information despite appearing not to do so. Learning from this, parents should continue to educate about sexuality even if children are non-verbal.

- See sex in the context of a range of activities their children might engage in.

- Establish foundations of sense of self, self-esteem and self-determination before tackling information about the specifics of sex.

- The usual rules apply: consistent, brief and simple information, repeated often and using different everyday contexts to reinforce the teaching. For example, if they are in a furniture store, reinforce that the beds are not in their children's bedroom, so their children cannot masturbate on them.

- Use of explicit, visual, symbols and language, repeatedly and opportunistically rehearsing, small, manageable parts.

Parents of autistic children are often used to explicitly and repeatedly teaching their children about what might be considered 'ordinary' daily activities of life, such as hand-washing or dressing. It is important to repeat information because some autistic children forget what they have been told while others need repetition to grasp concepts in the first place. Sex education for these children is an extension of that and there are resources available to help parents (see Resources).

Perhaps the greatest challenge is how parents feel about giving explicit information about sex to their children, especially those of the opposite gender, and what they need to know. Many parents feel they didn't 'sign up' for this when they entered parenthood, because sex education is often given at school, with additional information being derived from friends. Some parents feel inadequate or unprepared to engage in these discussions with their children, or may question the validity of teaching sex to moderately or severely autistic children.

Pet Names

Pet names such as 'front bottom', 'Mary', 'girlie bits' or 'down below' are not useful for girls, particularly because other adults may use different terms. This might not seem important now, but remember that parents are preparing their children for when the parents are no longer able to care for them and their children will be supported by other caregivers or health professionals. Parents should use the word 'vagina'.

For boys, the words 'willy', 'dick', 'cock' or even 'the old man' (imagine how the child might become confused with that last phrase) may be used by non-spectrum kids, but they will also learn the correct terminology. Severely autistic children need to know the 'proper' word, 'penis', which can be used in all circumstances. It may be important for these children to explain if they are unwell, or if they have been sexually abused, for example.

Non-Spectrum Phrases or Words

'Whoopy' or 'shagging' may be used by non-spectrum children and adults, but for those on the spectrum these phrases require a lot of explanation and learning when the correct terminology of 'sexual intercourse' and a clear explanation of what that means are what is needed by autistic kids. If parents are outlining a specific type of sexual intercourse, again, they should be accurate, for instance 'anal intercourse', 'vaginal intercourse' or 'oral sex'.

Use of symbols, such as Rebus or Makaton, is often a fundamental and early part of our children's education and ability to communicate. Symbols can be used to enhance our children's self-esteem, if used to communicate their opinions or choices about situations. They can be used to ensure inclusion of our children and consequently can improve confidence. There are some symbols cards depicting sexuality and its many aspects, which are commercially available (see Resources). Creating a communication book of symbols, which has symbols and their names which are bespoke for your children, can be extremely helpful to increase the relevance of any teaching to children's lives.

Visual Approaches

Visual approaches, such as social stories (Gray 2000), tend to work best with autistic children, whose verbal abilities frequently are delayed and/or they find the spoken word difficult to process and respond to. Social stories can help severely autistic children understand consequences of their actions, as well as thought processes and feelings associated with scenarios. This can be particularly useful when parents are working through issues about respect for self and others and enabling their children to know that others may think and feel differently from them.

Sometimes severely autistic children need pictures to be drawn specifically for them, either with their own picture stuck to a body or a drawing that they instantly recognise as themselves. This will enable them to understand that the story or information you are giving is relevant to them. Photographing familiar items, places or people who are relevant to their lives can enable their understanding, for example, a photograph of children's own bedrooms will illustrate where they can masturbate better than a picture of a generic bedroom from a magazine. The latter might lead children to believe that any bedroom setting is appropriate for masturbation, including a furniture shop's display of bedroom furniture. Others need the 'distance' of reading about a scenario which does not involve them. Parents will know if they can apply the story to what they do in reality. It is useful for the child if parents liaise with school to ensure consistency.

Of the available visual resources, Tissot's (2009) research found that some had brightly coloured backgrounds and too much text, which distracted children. Other resources had stick men which were understandable but did not have an anatomically correct drawing of a male erection. Parents may need to research which will most help them explain sex to their children and consider how much they may need to adapt the available resources for their use.

Magazines and newspapers can be helpful as visual aids. For example, parents can cut out images depicting different emotions to work out which emotion is shown with their children, then label the emotion on the picture. Parents can use these to enable their children to express their own emotions and keeping the list of emotions and pictures close to hand, so they become a resource. Parents may wish to extend this to their children painting or drawing their own 'list' of emotions.

Another idea would be to observe pictures of social situations which might stimulate discussion of emotions and could lead on to teaching about other important areas, such as what are appropriate public and private behaviours. For example, images of a couple kissing, fondling or having sexual intercourse would be useful materials to examine in this context. Indeed the concept of 'public' and 'private' can be illustrated with these photos.

Videos and some software programmes can similarly be used to try to initiate some thoughts about emotions or issues related to sex education. Many autistic children love 'screen' activities, so they will be engaged. The tricky part for parents of trying to 'ad lib' with resources is that many parents feel unable to discuss sex effectively and feel a need for absolute guidance as to what to say to their children.

Feedback from children will demonstrate if they understand what they have been taught by their parents. This could range from pictures or showing young people how to do something with actions, such as putting a condom on a banana or putting a sanitary towel into underwear to demonstrate knowledge and skills. Any information that parents explore with their children need to be repeated at intervals to ensure their children have absorbed it. If parents are about to build on previous information, it is helpful to revisit it to make sure their children have retained these foundations.

Another major consideration is communicating with their children's schools and other services that have involvement with their children to ensure they are aware of the boundaries parents set and the information parents are giving and this is supported and reinforced by these institutions. Parents may need to negotiate or glean advice from these professionals as well. For example, a parent may wish their child to be allowed to masturbate in school lavatories if/when the child becomes aroused in school time, so that the child does not feel this activity is 'wrong'. However, a school might have a policy of no masturbation whatsoever in school and would show picture jigs or otherwise reinforce that this behaviour is for the child's bedroom at home only. For other issues such as frottage (rubbing genitals against another person, usually through clothes), you may want to liaise about which picture jigs, social stories or comic strips are used, so the same ones are used in school and at home.

SENSE OF SELF

It is argued that 'sense of self' is the most basic and therefore the most important plank of education in sexuality (Hatton and Tector 2010). This phrase means guiding children to a point where they understand they are a separate entity to the parent or primary caregiver and in a broader sense they have self-awareness, including physically and emotionally being able to identify how they are or feel. This may start at a rudimentary level with enabling children to understand and acknowledge enjoying something as simple as the feel of a very soft, fluffy object, running water or the sun on their skin. This is a sense of self-awareness which can be celebrated and developed.

In non-spectrum children this sense is palpable when they start to be self-determining, whether this is in choosing clothing, food or television programmes, for example. They see themselves as individuals, apart from their caregivers, often indeed at odds with caregivers in asserting themselves. Of course, this is more marked when non-spectrum children become teenagers and appear (at least to their weary parents) to be trying to mark their 'difference' continuously and make strides in establishing themselves as self-determined, independent human beings.

In severely autistic children this sense of self may not develop to any extent 'naturally'. Parents need to encourage its development using exercises.

Mirror Games

Mirrors are useful props. Parents should make sure they use ones that are big enough for children to see both themselves and the parent. It is never too late to try these games, but the sooner the better. Parents usually are the best people to assess which games their children will be able to engage in, but my experience shows that schools can often engage autistic children in exercises and games that they won't attempt at home.

GROUND RULES FOR MIRROR GAMES

- Try to move on to other mirror games once the child feels comfortable with one game.

- Some autistic children may need to continuously start with a familiar game before they can progress onto others in any one mirror session.

- If the child is frightened of mirrors or unused to them, start with a small hand mirror and build up to larger mirrors.

- Some children on the spectrum find eye contact scary and can fight to avoid it. If this is the case, there is no need to make eye contact in the mirror. Instead, make the focus on mouths, whole face or specific external object, depending on which exercise you are doing.

- If the autistic child is likely to head butt or otherwise damage a mirror, with potential to damage themselves, use a non-glass mirror.

EXERCISE ONE

1. Parent is in front of a mirror with the child.

2. Parent touches their own face, smiles, winks, does something.

3. Parent encourages their child to do the same with their own face.

4. Parent uses simple words to establish 'my/Mum's/Dad's face' then 'your/child's name's face' to reinforce verbally that the faces are separate.

5. If the child is unable to engage at this level, try following your child's lead in using the mirror.

6. So if the child leans into the mirror, making sounds, do likewise. This is the essence of using 'intensive interaction' (see below), when non-spectrum educators meet the child at his/her level.

EXERCISE TWO

1. In non-verbal children or those with little verbalisation, the parent demonstrates different sounds and words by talking into the mirror. Parents may be surprised how little they open their mouths and how this may be difficult for their child to understand how to make different sounds which make up words.

2. Encourage the child to copy mouth shapes and sounds.

3. If a sound is created in the throat, encourage the child to feel the parent's neck where the sound is made, then feel their own neck as they try to make the same sound.

EXERCISE THREE

1. Put a small blob of cream or similar on the parent's own face somewhere obvious.

2. Share the mirror with the child and draw the child's attention to the blob, then remove it, showing the child as you do so.

3. Put a small blob of cream or similar on the child's face (somewhere obvious, nose, cheek, for example).

4. See if the child can spot the cream and touch or remove it.

EXERCISE FOUR

1. Encourage the child to try to wash their face, while watching their own actions in a mirror.

2. If the child cannot independently wash their face (yet), help them, but use the mirror.

3. It may help if the parent washes their own face first, while the child observes by looking at the reflection.

The Child in Context

Parents can help their children place themselves in the context of the family by using photographs.

1. Copy a series of photographs of the child from babyhood onwards to the current age. Make sure these are copies because parents probably will need to repeat this exercise at intervals or as time progresses for them to fully understand the concept of their own ageing and development.

2. Ask the child, using whatever method of communication they can access, who is on the photographs. If the parent includes a very recent shot, the child may immediately answer about that photograph at least.

3. Depending on how able the child is, the parent can ask them or help them put the photographs in age order from babyhood to present day. The parent can use repeated phrases to tell the

child this is a process of maturing, such as 'You are a baby on this picture, then you're getting older on this picture, then you're older...' The parent could place the photos on pegs in the child's bedroom or play area, so the child can review them. This concept of maturing is essential as a building block for parents to explain developing into adolescence and those changes. It is also fundamentally important to explain ageing, old age and dying as a cycle of life.

4. Use copies of photographs of other members of the family to show where the child 'fits', such as being the youngest or middle child. The child can gain the concept of having older and younger siblings, that the parent is older and grandparents are older still.

The Autistic Self

Some parents question the value of informing their own children that they have autism and what this might imply for their future lives. This is particularly the case with severely autistic children, in my experience. This is when it is useful to learn from higher functioning autistic people who can articulate the importance of this aspect of awareness of self, which informs them:

- why they find change hard to manage

- why they feel angry and frustrated so often

- that others cannot readily understand what they do and why

- that they are different.

This understanding can reduce anxieties and is enabling. Acknowledging that severely autistic children are different gives them permission to explore how others behave and how they themselves behave; it validates their existence as a different person. Knowledge can enable our children to learn about appropriate ways to express anger, sadness or joy, for example, so that these emotions are understood by others. Ignoring that our children have autism can undermine their development of sense of self and, in effect, will be disabling.

The above exercises are not exhaustive. The important point is to gradually reinforce and establish in the child's mind that they are not the same person as the parent. For some children, this may take little time, for others it may take months. But understanding that they are separate entities to the parent is a fundamental foundation on which to build self-esteem, self-determination and other key elements that are essential to creating a robust personality.

SELF-ESTEEM

Self-esteem is defined as valuing oneself for who you are and what you like or what interests you. In severely autistic children, it may be difficult to assess levels of self-esteem, which may become an issue only when children's behaviours indicate that there is a lack of self-esteem. For example, if an autistic child is self-injurious, there may be other causes but one may be lack of self-esteem, leading to lack of self-determination and frustration.

If a child engages continuously in 'stimming' (self-stimulatory behaviours) or is non-verbal, for instance, parents may feel that there is no route for enhancing self-esteem or maybe no worth in trying. I would argue that bolstering self-esteem reduces the likelihood of what are perceived to be 'vulnerable' people being sexually abused. In addition, parents never know how far their children will develop and self-esteem is crucial to their children establishing friendships. Whether or not they are able to take this one step further to romantic relationships (even if no actual sexual contact is involved), self-esteem is a basis for this to happen in a safer way for autistic children because self-esteem increases children's assertion skills.

Intensive Interaction and 'Joining'

Intensive interaction is credited with building self-esteem by giving the child the lead in interactions and by appreciating and endorsing the child's preferences for activities (Nind and Hewett 2001). It is very similar to the term 'joining' used in the Son-Rise programme (see Resources). Some music therapists work in similar ways, to give the child the ability to direct the pace and volume of music and which instruments are played during a session. These approaches set value by the child's own inherent strengths and interests without setting goals of changing the child's focus.

It may seem odd if a child is severely autistic to talk of 'strengths and interests'. For many parents, a child who rocks endlessly, or makes sounds which are incomprehensible as words or approximations of words, may seem beyond any notions of 'interests'. Yet this approach is precisely aimed at appreciating whatever a child presents with, whether parents understand the motivation behind actions, whether they would choose to do particular things, or not.

The use of 'deep pressure' is also a means of communicating and building self-esteem at a level which reaches severely autistic children. Exercises involve squeezing balls which increases the proprioceptive input, that is, the body's automatic way of interpreting its position and movement (see Appendix 2) which therefore reduces children's anxieties. Another route is experiencing trust and developing relationships with a child by sitting back to back rocking side to side, feeling the pressure against each other while mirroring the child's movements. The child gains a sense of how it feels when their body moves in space as well as the intimacy of being close without the pressure to make eye contact; finally they lead the exercise because the parent is copying what they do.

Stimming's implicit purpose is usually to increase sensory input to children whose autism causes them to lack it. Some ASD children are the opposite and feel overwhelmed by sensory stimuli when doing 'ordinary' things such as shopping in a supermarket, so their sensitivities often lead to emotional outbursts.

Sometimes parents see the purpose of behaviours only by doing them themselves. Intensive interaction and joining give parents the experience their children have, while validating their behaviours. When I worked with my son, I had no understanding of his actions. His days were filled by holding innumerable pencils or pens or a CD in each hand before his eyes. It was only when I copied precisely what he did that I found he only held the 'rainbow' side of a CD to his face and watched the colours as he rotated the CD in his hands. He very dextrously held the pencils and pens and rotated them, too. In mimicking him, I found the activity extremely absorbing to the point where I could see how it distracted him and removed him from the rest of the social world. In doing so, the behaviour soothed him. No amount of interruptions would distract him from stimming until I mirrored him; for the first time he stopped, looked at what I was doing then looked at my face.

With verbal autistic children, parents are encouraged to show interest in their children's 'special interest' as a way of valuing them as people. This is equally as valid when working with non-verbal, less communicative autistic children but their interests may feel more obscure or nebulous to us; it is only by engaging in their world that parents understand what these children are experiencing and why they behave as they do.

SELF-DETERMINATION

An integral part of joining or intensive interaction is allowing the child to take the lead in any activity. This is potentially very challenging for parents who may be used to being in control and may have little trust of the autistic person to know what they want, particularly if the child has few skills with which to communicate. It is much faster, more efficient for parents to take over and may feel more comfortable to them. However, if the overarching goal of parents is to enable their children to be as independent as possible for when their parents are no longer here, it is critical that parents pull back and invest trust in their children to enable them to develop skills, including a level of self-determination.

As a term, self-determination is a process of asserting oneself. Ultimately the goal is to enable children to make choices about their lives, including sexuality. This might mean a decision about their own bodies, such as whether or not to engage in sexual activity, or have treatment for a testicular or breast tumour. It might mean them assessing risks around sexual behaviours and keeping safe.

In my experience of autism parents, there appear to be two camps regarding self-determination as a concept for severely autistic children. One says that they can never achieve any meaningful level of self-determination. The other camp states that family life has been utterly dominated by their autistic children's self-determination. To the latter, I would caution not to confuse self-determination with wilfulness, which may be born of a need to pit against being told what to do, in essence having no self-determination being the root cause of these behaviours. To the first argument I would say that any measure of self-determination is worth targeting and that we cannot calculate how much our children will develop and over how long a period. Certainly, our children may take different paths to non-spectrum children to socially develop, but our children do continue developing well into adulthood. Non-spectrum adults also develop too, of course, but they have usually achieved the basics of social communication when they enter adulthood while our children will continue to tackle these.

Self-determination is best encouraged early and over small matters initially, just the same as with non-spectrum children. One major area to work on is hygiene and dressing. Often, using a full-length mirror can be useful (allowing for any potential to harm themselves or others if using a glass mirror). So parents can work with their children to allow them to choose cloths for washing or towels (according to colour, size or softness), soaps (hard or liquid) or sponges. Parents should ensure those choices are real, that is, they have a range to choose from. They can also reinforce their children's choices verbally and, of course, by ensuring they can actualise their choices. Parents can encourage use of the mirror, so children see themselves washing, and removing dirt from their faces, for example. Another crucial element of self-care is to ensure as soon as possible that children do not rely on others for intimate care, which leaves them more open to sexual abuse. Of course, some severely autistic children will continue to need support to wash, dress and use the lavatory. For them it is important that they become aware that only certain adults give them such care. It is vital to increase their abilities to self-care as far as possible for their own self-esteem and self-determination and to reduce their dependence on others.

With clothes, parents can encourage their children to choose from a range of what they want to wear. But it has to be a real choice. There is little point presenting only what parents want them to be seen in, or letting children choose then dressing them in what parents feel comfortable with. One woman I worked with allowed her daughter to 'choose' clothes, 'so long as they didn't make her look stupid', then was surprised when the girl wouldn't help dress herself, even though the mother was aware she could when she liked what she was going to wear. My son adores shirts and ties, but he will never tuck in a shirt and insists on men's shirts; he can say about boys' shirts 'they too small'. In fact they are his size, but they are fitted when he clearly likes his clothes loose. He leaves our house wearing track suit bottoms, men's shirts and ties, often topped with a waistcoat. He does look different from non-spectrum children of his age. Perhaps he is open to being laughed or stared at. My argument is that his behaviours alone might induce the same reaction from non-spectrum observers. In himself, though, he appears confident in his outfits, frequently stopping to admire himself in shop windows. By letting him wear what he wants, he will dress himself without qualm and I am validating his choice above anything I might want. He also learns that he cannot always have his choices when he goes to school, for instance, when he must wear uniform. This is an important boundary for him.

Creating an environment for self-determination entails loosening control and sometimes standing back while offspring do things parents would rather they didn't. Another mother, for example, was annoyed with the special needs school for letting her daughter wear her sweater inside out after a swimming lesson. The child had dressed herself, but the mother found it unacceptable that staff hadn't made her daughter take off the sweater and replace it without the seams showing. The triumph that the girl had dressed herself was swallowed up by the annoyance (not to say anger) that the mother felt towards what she felt was negligence. The girl's mother went on to tell me that she knew her daughter would never manage to dress herself properly and here was the proof; from that point onwards she made sure she dressed her daughter so she looked 'normal' in public.

This desire to protect her daughter (and possibly herself) from ridicule completely undermined not only her daughter's independence but also her self-esteem and ability to practise self-determination. Many very young non-spectrum children who are learning to dress themselves will roll out of school after games wearing several things inside out or back-to-front; it is part of the process of acquiring dressing skills to get it 'wrong'. What that mother could constructively have done was to help her daughter by using a full-length mirror to ask what might make her outfit better and look carefully at how her daughter might learn that the seams go on the inside, bearing in mind that the very reason the girl might leave seams on the outside is that they might feel 'bumpy' or uncomfortable. If that is the case, it is a matter of finding clothes that the daughter likes to wear the correct way round on her body.

Self-determination is a process, rather than an entity. As it develops, autistic children will gain the insight that they have a say in what happens. Parents need to include in the experience of self-determination that their children have an opportunity to say 'no' to things. Parents can start small with food choices, for example, when their children learn that saying 'no' has a positive impact for them in that they are taken seriously. Parents can expand their children's opportunities to use 'no' and adhere to what they say. There is a real argument for teaching negotiation and compromise to our children, rather than instilling a culture of compliance.

In terms of sexuality, saying 'no' and being heard is critical. Empowering autistic children to say 'no' to unwanted touch may sound obvious. However, culturally many people expect children to endure hugs and kisses from relatives or friends, which are non-sexual, but unwanted. Parents need to encourage children to refuse unwanted contact and ensure this is acted on. This increases children's self-belief that when they say 'no' that is precisely what is heard and will cause the consequence they ask for. Starting when they are very young, or when they start to have any progress in social communication, parents can play low level games which introduce the idea of turn-taking, give and take, and giving and receiving consent.

CIRCLES OF CONNECTIONS AND CONTACTS

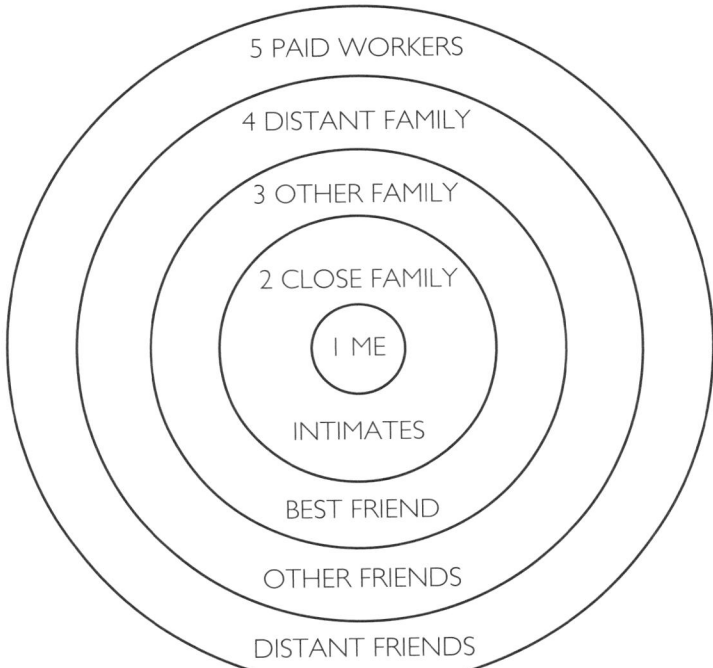

Figure 1 Circles of connections and contacts or 'My Social Circles'

Source: Adapted from original concepts by Walker-Hirsch and Champagne (1991) and Stanfield (undated)

The concept of circles of connections and contacts can be used in many ways (see Figure 1). It is best to personalise it visually by naming it 'My Social Circles' and using children's names or sticking photographs of children in the 'Me' circle, so they recognise it is pertinent to their lives. Parents can portray this as a 'live' concept, in which people can move into and out of circles and the rights and responsibilities these circles give them. The idea of these circles is well established in sexuality teaching, with some people using colours, names and/or numbers to delineate between circles. For example, circle 1 in yellow might be the 'hugging' circle. For some severely autistic children, these extra prompts might enable their learning but for many children, colours may distract and numbers or names may be beyond their cognitive abilities at that point. So for many children, a black and white diagram with a picture or symbol of how to greet others, or what their roles are in children's lives, will be sufficient. Photographs of contacts in each of the circles is a highly visual and helpful way of communicating with more cognitively impaired children.

Circles of connections and contacts can be used to examine the different ways we should greet people in our lives. Unless they are clearly informed via picture jigs, stories or verbally, autistic children will not discern between those who can expect a more intimate greeting, such as a hug, and those whose hands might be shaken or given a 'high five' (a common greeting these days). The diagram can visually show the child how greetings become more formal the further away from the child the person is on the circles.

The 'Me' circle could contain the child's abilities, such as 'I can wash myself' and 'I can touch myself'. It could list activities the child likes to do or preferences, so my son's would have said 'I like straight things, like pencils and straws' when he was first diagnosed as being autistic.

The next circle of close family and intimates could have photographs and names of all those in the family who give intimate care, such as the parents. In some families this may also be the grandparents. If the 'child' is in a consensual sexual relationship, this person should be in this circle. The circle should contain a statement that the child can say 'no' to sexual activity or touching and the person addressed will stop. It is also important to state how the child should greet these people (a hug and a kiss is usual).

Parents should work through all circles, with particular reference to how to greet and who should touch the child and how (a 'high five' is a touch, after all). It is vital to explain that some paid workers may be greeted by a handshake but may need to examine or touch private body parts, for example, doctors. Outside these circles are 'strangers' who are people the child has not met or been introduced to. Some of these strangers can be talked to in very specific circumstances, such as police officers if the child is lost or scared.

For prevention of sexual abuse, remember that most children are not abused by strangers; they know their abusers. This diagram can help children understand who should be close to them physically – 'within arm's length' – and who should not.

Touch is often an area which autistic people find confusing, even unpredictable and therefore frightening, due to sensory issues. Hatton and Tector's (2010) study found that intense concerns about touch resulted in some severely autistic adults needing to be totally in control of any sexual touching, while others refused any form of sexual touch by others and focused on solo sexual behaviours only (Hatton and Tector 2010). It is part of sexuality teaching that should be explored, using notions of 'private body zones' and 'good touch, bad touch'.

This will help children to identify when someone is behaving inappropriately. This needs to be supported by friends, who may feel they are being unkind to a severely autistic child if they refuse a hug, for example. Family and other caregivers also need to understand the purpose and necessity of adhering to these boundaries.

Different circles denote different behaviours. It is important that friends and family agree to adhere with the rules of intimacy that parents discuss with their children, otherwise they can confuse autistic children, who need clear, unequivocal parameters to follow. As an example, I am aware of a friend who consistently allows someone's severely autistic adult son to rest his head on her shoulder and sit very close to her on a sofa. This feels comfortable to her because she has known him since he was a baby, and clearly it is to him, since he initiates the contact. Now imagine that man on a bus, seeing a woman who looks like the warm friend of his mother's, for example. His behaviour is likely to be the same as when he's at home with the friend. He may lean up against the stranger, resting his head on her – and landing himself in trouble with the police or, at the very least, getting thrown off the bus without any understanding as to what he has done wrong.

To mould appropriate behaviours, parents need to imagine our children in different scenarios behaving the way they do at home. Severely autistic children have extreme difficulty differentiating between what is appropriate in one setting as opposed to another.

They tend to apply behaviours practised at home in the public arena, so parents must ensure those behaviours are appropriate. Often, a way of conveying the importance is to say how children's understanding and use of boundaries will protect them from abuse and allow them to indicate more easily if abuse has taken place using a circles of connections and contacts chart.

Although they may not raise the alarm to this, parents can regularly go through the circles of connections and contacts to ensure that a person who should be on one of the outer circles is not suddenly appearing in their children's eyes in an inner circle of closeness. Bear in mind that this may reflect the children's desires that particular people are in the inner circle, so parents should not assume abuse but investigate further with their children.

Building on concepts involved in circles of connections and 'public versus private' (see below) parents need to reinforce that there are private body parts. One strategy is to have a drawing showing 'zones' or areas which no one other than their child should touch without the child's permission. It may be helpful to draw the clothes that go over the body parts, too. So, for example, the child may learn that no other person should touch the area where their underpants are without permission. This includes touching through clothing.

This diagram is also helpful for trying to prevent children being abducted by someone who might tempt autistic children away with their favourite subject. For example, if a child is fascinated by a particular sporting celebrity, parents can discuss who else might know about that celebrity (most of the general public, located in the very outer circle of 'strangers'). The rules about not talking to strangers still apply, even if someone knows a great deal about the child's special subject. By visualising that someone is on the outer circle, despite knowing about the child's celebrity interest, the child can picture the physical distance to keep from this stranger and not be drawn into confidences with a stranger by virtue of what seems to be a shared interest.

Parents can discuss who should have intimate knowledge of their children's bodies, relating this to whatever stage they have reached in naming body parts, intimate washing and drying tasks or public versus private behaviours. This may lead to examining friendships and relationships, teaching how to fill a circle with these and how intimate these might be.

Another use of circles of connections and contacts is to develop an idea of what is appropriate touching for different people within the different circles. These can be put together in a book for children to refer to. It is clear that the larger the circle of contacts the child has, the less opportunity for sexual abuse to take place and the greater the likelihood that it will be discovered if it does occur. Remember that sexual abuse is overwhelmingly inflicted by people the child knows, not opportunistically by a stranger. There are also resources about appropriate and inappropriate touch (Manasco and Manasco 2012).

FRIENDSHIPS

Friendships and social contacts are fundamentally important to the psychological well-being of severely autistic children. Families cannot provide the complete social network these children need to develop to their full potential socially. If parents are to support their children adequately, they need to nourish and help maintain their children's friendships by providing transport, supporting their children going to events with friends or having friends stay overnight, even if this may mean that parents temporarily have responsibility for another severely autistic person. This can feel tremendously onerous for exhausted parents, especially if their children's friends have additional conditions, such as epilepsy, which can start in around a quarter of severely autistic children as they reach adolescence (Edelson 2011). Parents may have to learn how to manage seizures in other children, if not in their own (see Appendix 3).

Non-spectrum children can create and maintain friendships and can and do move onto new friendships with relative ease. Autistic children cannot. The few friendships they make are precious and I feel that it is parents' duty to foster these social contacts. Many such friendships are curtailed when these children leave school and are allocated different educational establishments or residential units. All the social investment they have made and the regular experience of seeing familiar faces and socially interacting with them can be dashed, leaving them grieving for friendships. Parents need to anticipate these changes and facilitate their children's friendships.

Without sufficient support to enable children to develop and maintain friendships, parents leave them open to possible abuse of various sorts. If severely autistic children become lonely or recognise their difference from other non-spectrum adults, they can be more easily manipulated by abusive others in their desperation to be liked or feel they have a friendship. If parents don't teach their children about what constitutes a healthy friendship, children will not understand when they are being emotionally or sexually abused for the benefit of others. If parents aren't explicit about what is sexual behaviour, autistic children may behave sexually towards others because this behaviour appears to be creating friendships; in reality their actions are allowing them to be variously abused in their bid for companionship.

Even severely autistic children may sense that they are not like other people, yet still want relationships without the coaching and knowledge that non-spectrum others have around issues such as dress codes, appropriate touch and body space. Giving these children opportunities to experience friendships, with all the mistakes that can happen in communication and the need to develop understanding of another's perspective, will enable them to create and maintain relationships if that possibility arises. Knowing the mechanics of sex and physical changes involved in adolescence is not enough to enable such children to make safe and healthy sexual decisions or be aware when something is happening which is ethically wrong.

PUBLIC VERSUS PRIVATE

Public versus private is a critical concept for autistic children to grasp because their understanding will help prevent them doing activities in public that could cause them to be put on the sex offenders' register. Although the law will take account of children's autism, certain sexual behaviours in public are an offence, and intellectual disability, like ignorance, is no defence. It is up to parents to inform their children about what is appropriate or not in public, to protect them and members of society.

Private can be described as being alone in a place where no one else can see them or interrupt them. This would be the children's bedroom. Often a photograph of their bedroom is the way to accurately convey that it is only this room that is private. One concern is that some autistic children are shown the generic symbols for 'private' on a door to depict that it is not a public place. However, these symbols are also commonly seen on signs, for example, on doors in shops and offices which clearly are not private in the sense that people can masturbate in them. This is another reason why it is wise to designate children's bedrooms as the only private place for masturbation.

Parents could describe a public place as somewhere that anyone can go and where their children will not be alone and where other people will see them. It is always a good idea to give examples which children are familiar with or use photographs. This learning can be reinforced in daily living by restating which places are public when you are in them, such as the shops or in the street.

I often read about or answer questions from parents who consider a bathroom or lavatory to be a private place and describe it as such to their autistic offspring. In some ways these locations may seem private but from a perspective of sexuality, they hold significant problems. If autistic children need assistance with intimate personal care from others, such as washing, this is likely to take place in a lavatory or bathroom. So it is not an appropriate place to encourage masturbation from the perspective of preventing sexual abuse or protecting staff or others giving intimate care.

Part of the rationale behind teaching the private and public lesson is to ensure that autistic children do not perform private activities in public places. Yet lavatories are public places and children may not differentiate between a lavatory at home and one in a shopping centre. If autistic children masturbate in a public place, even behind a closed door, this is an offence.

Parents also have to ask themselves if they want their children to be masturbating (this being an obviously private behaviour) in a bathroom at home, when:

- others could need the lavatory

- others might interrupt and upset our sons by knocking on the door

- where our sons might feel rushed and unable to reach climax, leading to frustration

- they may not clean up after themselves if hurried.

Parents should be wary of symbols which show the sign 'private' on a door; there are many such signs on doors in shops and offices and their children may not differentiate between these two locations if they are following what they have been taught on a sign.

A second major reason for teaching about private and public is in relation to body parts when these children need to learn that their genitalia are private body parts which remain hidden and personal unless they are in an intimate relationship with another person, who agrees with showing private body parts. This is an important concept to prevent frottage (rubbing or thrusting genitalia against another person) and is closely linked with work around circles of intimacy and who can be physically close and see private body parts.

Specifically for females, they need to understand that breasts as well as the vagina and buttocks/bottom are considered 'private' parts of the body. This may need clarifying when it comes to the case of nursing mothers, who may be subtle, but autistic women may notice 'displaying' breasts in a public place such as a cafe or park. Parents should ensure that their children know this is the only time when breasts may be visible because they are being used to feed a baby and the mother will be trying to keep her breasts covered as much as possible.

Whatever parents' feelings about their autistic children maturing in to adults, they will physically do so, regardless of mental capacity to deal with relationships or emotions. This can be extremely difficult for parents to accept. They may have a child who has started menstruating or has pubic hair, yet still plays in the bath with young children's toys or watches toddlers' videos. Trying to instil rules around sleeping, touch, dressing or nudity can feel inappropriate for a 'child' who doesn't display the mental maturity which fits their physical appearance.

Non-spectrum children naturally withdraw from their parents around adolescence and even fight for a feeling of independence and separation as they establish themselves as individuals. Parents have to adapt to this, usually through a period of mourning, especially when children leave home and create an independent home leaving an empty nest.

Children on the extreme end of the autism spectrum do not often experience this rite of passage. Parents may find they have to do work with the child for the child to gain a sense of self, apart from the primary caregiver. Without this removal of emotional ties and absolute level of dependence, children cannot establish themselves and be enabled to progress onto forging other relationships.

Learning about relationships is a complex process which cannot be completed in any neat parcel when we work with autistic children. The knowledge and skills involved are developed over years – some would argue over the entire lifetime – the seeds of which are sown in early childhood (Hatton and Tector 2010). For autistic children with profound communication difficulties, parents may feel that there is a delay in teaching them about developing relationships, but by ongoing relationships with their children, parents are a constant source of teaching for them. Although children on the autism spectrum may not learn efficiently through 'osmosis' or non-specific observation of peers, they do learn in the family environment, watching repeated behaviours of others.

If autistic children are brought up in violent or angry households, this is what those children will learn is appropriate with other humans and will copy. Equally if children experience sexual abuse, they will interpret that as acceptable behaviour with others. Autistic children are notably literal and view situations in black and white terms as being wholly right or wrong, so poor examples in the home environment will be reflected in their adult behaviours unless there is some intervention or work done with the individual.

It is critical that there are clear, unequivocal house rules which reinforce the notion of privacy, of correct attire in public areas in the home, of bedrooms as being private – and one's own bedroom being the *only* place to practise masturbation. The impact of poor boundaries and lack of privacy, for example, with family members wandering about the house naked or not knocking on bedroom doors, can create an impression on autistic children that nowhere is private, so they can access any area without asking and that clothing is optional. This is also an important concept in residential settings, where lack of privacy and respect for personal space by knocking on bedroom doors is lamentably poor (Hollomotz 2011).

Parents' behaviours at home and the rules they apply to their children will shape their ability to manage in the absence of their parents in future. One of the key principles in educating children about sex is the concept of public and private behaviours. How parents conduct themselves will be observed by their children and copied, especially if behaviours are repeated and therefore embedded in their children's minds as 'acceptable'. If parents wander about the house naked, if they don't knock on bedroom doors, if they leave bathroom doors open, their children will see this as acceptable behaviour. Their children will not differentiate behaviours and understand that when the household has visitors, parents do not wander around naked and do lock bathroom doors, for example. Autistic children who do not learn firm rules around private activities and public ones will prevent siblings being able to invite friends back, for fear of the autistic child's behaviours. Contrary to what I see on my and other websites, this lack of knowledge and inappropriate behaviour is not the 'fault' of autism which is inflicted on the child. It is a palpable lack of education on the part of parents or primary caregivers, whose responsibility it is to give their autistic children guidance as to what is and is not acceptable both in words and in modelling good behaviours.

Single parent families also have to have some discussion with the other parent, if they share the children's time at all. This can be difficult if the separation was hostile. I am aware of one example when the estranged husband and his new partner lived together and clearly were used to wandering naked in their house, which they continued when the severely autistic son stayed there. In addition, the son shared a double bed with his sister, who was developing sexually. The mother was told of the situation by the daughter, who had just started her periods and was still expected to sleep with her brother. The strained relationships between the parents caused the father to refuse to comply with the mother's requests for no nudity and separate beds for the children. Ultimately it took counselling intervention to stop these practices. It is worth noting that in this example, the mother knew of the problem only because her daughter was able to inform her; the son was non-verbal.

These rules should be agreed by all family or friends who might care for the children. When separations between partners cause conflict, it is sometimes helpful to use a professional who doesn't have a bias, only the child's interests, to move scenarios forward.

House Rules

House rules should include the following:

- Knock on 'private' doors such as bedrooms and await instructions or acknowledgement which parents can script. For example, 'Who is it?' then 'Yes, you can come in.' Parents need to remember that they have to follow the same rules, so they must knock and await the scripted response before they enter their child's bedroom. (If parents aren't at a point where their ASD child can lock the door for safety reasons, see below.)

- Undress or dress in bedrooms or the bathroom with the doors shut. No wandering around the house (even just upstairs) naked or just in underwear unless it is in one's own bedroom with the door shut.

- All masturbation in the individual's own bedroom only.

- Use the bathroom or toilet with the door locked. If parents are concerned about their child getting locked in, they can have a lock fitted which can be unlocked from the outside in emergencies. As soon as is practical, children should be using the toilet without being observed by another: this is an important lesson for adulthood or when their children are using public lavatories. Parents should ensure that their children know that other older children and adults never need help with their intimate care or private parts.

- If their children are physically and mentally capable, parents should get them to wash and dress themselves as soon as practicable in their childhood. Removing this responsibility from able autistic children creates dependence on an adult, a routine which may be impossible to shift as parents get older. If parents die, this will leave their children more vulnerable.

- Separate bedrooms or certainly separate beds for children of different genders.

- No sexual activity which your children might observe.

- The 'arm's length bubble': parents should ensure that their children know that others who are not in their close circle (see 'Circles of connections and contacts' on page 59) should physically be an arm's length away from them, in a 'bubble' around the child. This provides a physical boundary which their children can easily create with their own arms, preserving their own and others' personal space, which can be a difficult concept for autistic children to grasp. This should be rehearsed at home.

The home environment should give children their sense of security and belonging. Sometimes it will not seem like this to parents when their children crash around, smashing up objects, screaming or otherwise acting out. Parents have to remember at these times that because their home gives their children a safe haven, they feel able to release emotion, even if it is not done constructively.

SLEEPING ARRANGEMENTS

Anywhere from 40 to 80 per cent of children across the autism spectrum have difficulty sleeping (Eggerding 2010).

Reasons for sleep problems include the following:

- Some autistic children produce insufficient melatonin, which is a hormone that regulates our sleeping patterns. In discussion with their child's medical consultant, parents may decide to give their child melatonin medication to improve sleep patterns. Personally, I keep all medications I give to either of my children to an absolute minimum because there are side-effects and long-term effects associated with all drugs, especially when dealing with children whose brains do not fully develop until their early twenties.

- Environmental factors can affect sleep, such as stimulating activities just prior to bedtime, or placing children to sleep in a room in which they usually do stimulating activities.

- Difficulties with social cueing are common in autism and mean that children don't easily learn the order in which things occur and don't make the link between the household going to bed and their own need and necessity to sleep.

- Sensory issues can cause problems with the process of falling asleep due to sensitivities to sounds, smells, sights and touch.

- Inadvertently moulding children's sleep patterns can create problems. For example, if children are rocked to sleep then placed in bed already asleep, when they naturally wake in the night (which we all do) they don't have the ability to return to sleep because the very thing that enables them to sleep is missing (the parents).

- Medical problems can interfere with sleep, such as night terrors, seizures and anxiety, all of which are relatively common in autism.

Parents may be unwilling to disclose information about their sleeping arrangements to professionals, for fear of some slur about sexual abuse or just general disapproval. Professionals may well ask parents to keep sleep diaries and this can be useful for working out strategies for how best to support their children. But sleep diaries are only as good as parents' incentive to use them.

Inwardly, parents know that their autistic children should be sleeping alone in their own beds in their own rooms. Certainly, this should be the case by the time these children are ten years old. I have experience of the difficulties parents can have with severely autistic young children. It is utterly exhausting to have a hyperactive, non-verbal child bashing around the home all day and often up most of the night doing the same. Parents are directed by professionals to use signing, symbols or pictures to help with communication, inundated with 'best practice' for every aspect of autism, while they struggle to form a sentence because they are so tired. So when it comes to sleeping arrangements, parents do whatever works best to get a few hours of sleep.

My experience with autism parents is that the 'breadwinner' is the priority in the sleep department. It is usually the father, who is given a bed where he is least likely to be disturbed, generally in a guest bedroom. If there is no spare bedroom, he may find he is tipped out of the marital bed in the night, due to force of numbers or drama as the mother tries to calm their autistic child. The occasional night in the parents' bed fast becomes a regular thing and we all know how autistic children like their routines. Parents quickly find they have a nightly episode of 'musical beds' where they start in one bed with one bedfellow and end up in another or with another.

For single mothers, it is even easier to slip into sleeping with their autistic children because they may not have to disturb a bedfellow. Depending on the level of practical support single parents receive, they may be even more tired than a married autism mother who can be relieved in parenting duties by the father.

Inappropriate sleeping arrangements are common in autism families and, in my experience, are caused by the following:

- Utter exhaustion, which is frequently at the heart of any poor decisions parents make about or for their autistic children.

- Parents' desperation for sleep.

- Autistic children may be more amenable to cuddles and closeness when sleeping, which parents often long for and don't achieve when the child's awake due to sensory issues.

- Misplaced tendency to prioritise the autistic child's needs above all other concerns. I would argue this is based on guilt.

- Parental 'carer's/caregiver's role', which creates social empathy and legitimises financial benefits we may receive from the state.

- Reluctance to engage in sexual behaviours with the other marital partner, so the autistic child provides a 'legitimate' barrier.

- A difficult marital relationship which may be exacerbated by the presence of autism in the family unit. The severely autistic child may at once be a cause of marital strife and the reason the marital partners feel obliged to stay together.

Most young autistic children are chaotic and hyperactive until the age of around eight years, regardless of where on the spectrum they ultimately end up. This is a tough and gruelling period for parents. It is also a time when poor sleeping arrangements become established.

What parents have to do is project their thoughts into the future and imagine their children in ten years' time. If their autistic son is nine years old today and sleeping with his mother on a nightly basis, is this appropriate when he's 19? What about when he's 30? What happens when he starts to masturbate?

It is hard to introduce change to routines, but here are a few ideas:

- Give plenty of notice of the changes. If parents can engage their children with books, find some that, in passing, show children in their own beds and bedrooms and draw their children's attention to this. Autistic children often want to be like non-spectrum 'ordinary' children.

- Parents can create a bedroom that their autistic child wants to be in. Lighting, music, lavender oil under the pillow, whatever helps their own child. This may involve what might seem bizarre props. For example, my son insisted on my pinning tatty pieces of card from food wrappers and scrappy, minute pictures to the walls. He also drew all over the door and walls.

- Draw pictures and social stories (Gray 2000) to explain about new sleeping routines and arrangements.

- Parents should consider activities before bedtime and count down stimulating play so that it ends an hour or so before bedtime and ensure this is included on any visual schedule or stories they use to explain what's going to happen.

- Initially it may be helpful to have a worn and physically soft item of the mother's clothing for the child to cuddle into – but parents should aim to withdraw this as soon as their child is into a routine of sleeping in their own bed and bedroom.

- Parents should not lock their children in their bedroom at night to enforce changes. Aside from the trauma this might cause children if they try to leave the room, for the lavatory or to join their parents, it is extremely dangerous if there is a fire when parents may be unable to release their child and they cannot escape.

- Parents might discuss with their children's doctor short-term use of melatonin or a sedative, until your child establishes the new sleeping routine.

- Parents need to be consistent and remember to think about ten years' time.

RESPECT FOR OTHERS

Some of these children's most important social lessons will be around emotions, which are the basis of any relationship and one of the hardest notions for severely autistic people to grasp. The place to start, of course, is with the child's own feelings and enabling such children to locate and identify feelings in themselves. Often, autistic children can appreciate physical effects of emotion, such as having a flushed face, sweaty hands and a bouncing heartbeat, but they do not recognise this as being anger, so they cannot name the feeling.

It is a long process which will help autistic children understand feelings they experience. This may involve identifying the physical signs for these children when parents see they are emotional and naming the feeling. This is most usefully followed up with picture jigs or photographs with the emotion named on it. As parents build up their children's repertoire of known emotions, parents can show them a series of 'feelings' cards depicting a range of emotions and get the children to select the one they are feeling. This can reduce misbehaviour which is often a means of more severely autistic children drawing attention to a need but without being able to identify and name what it is. Cards of feelings can facilitate this. My son's behaviours frequently become challenging when he's unwell. Even though he has some speech, it is limited and his ability to construct sentences is limited to a few words. Given feelings cards, he can readily show why he is misbehaving. Over time, he will become able to locate the feeling instead of having to act out for attention and understanding.

Severely autistic people may never truly 'live' an emotion in the sense that non-spectrum people do and may identify feelings at what might be considered an academic level, as an 'outsider'. However, this aspect of learning, like many others, can be taught so that our children have insights that help them manage better in the social world. If our children can identify when an emotion is building inside and what that emotion is, they can learn to express it in a way that non-spectrum others can understand rather than in what appear to be unanticipated, often frightening, outbursts. Strategies can be built in, to enable more severely autistic children to better manage feelings. In practice, this may be as rudimentary as holding up an emotions card when a situation is becoming too challenging or as complex as talking about feelings with a friend or sharing feelings when a person has been rejected in friendship or a relationship.

Only when our children can identify personal feelings will they be able to expand their social knowledge to begin to comprehend others' emotions and the significance of these. This is the foundation of understanding relationships and fundamentals such as power and how this is exercised.

Exercises to Learn about Respecting Others

Have pictures on cards of the six most basic of emotions, these being happy, sad, angry, afraid, surprised and disgusted. At home, parents can attribute these to members of the family as the day progresses, so their children understand that emotions change over time. Link the change in feelings to what has happened, using either social stories or comic strips, if their children can follow the 'action'. The latter are more helpful in explaining emotions because they contain the opportunity to attach feelings to characters.

The more specific parents can be in their information, the more likely their child will comprehend. So a photograph of the actual family member in question, linked directly with the emotion, is more helpful than a drawing of that person or just their name under a pin person. I would have a pile of scanned photos of the family, if possible pulling the faces of the basic emotions, which parents can utilise throughout the day. If the emotion is related to the actions of their children, parents can visually give examples to the child of choices they make or behaviours and how these can affect others as consequences. This is giving them a simplistic basis to start understanding relationships. These life lessons are easiest to learn at home, which is 'safe', in terms of relationships and familiar objects and facilities that can reduce anxieties in the child.

Once a child is familiar with emotions cards, parents can use them to identify feelings attributed to others when they broach other subjects such as private versus public behaviours. One element of this will involve discussing what impact doing private behaviours in public might have on others' feelings. Many severely autistic people may not have real insight into emotion, but they can learn that they are not to induce unwanted feelings in others. Just as parents will be teaching them that the rule around masturbation is 'only in your bedroom', these children can learn that there are rules around others' emotions.

Understanding that others have feelings and these may not be the same as theirs, these offspring gain some level of empathy. This will help them deal with rejection when friendships or possibly relationships don't work out. Rejection is an important area to explore because autistic children often invest in relationships when it is clear to non-spectrum people that there is no 'relationship' as such. This is partly born of these children's lack of natural empathic response and partly due to their need for companionship. When their physical advances are not reciprocated, this can lead such children to self-injurious, aggressive behaviours or a further withdrawal from the social world.

SEXUAL INTERCOURSE

The mechanics of sex should be taught only when other building blocks of understanding have been established. This is illustrated in Figure 2.

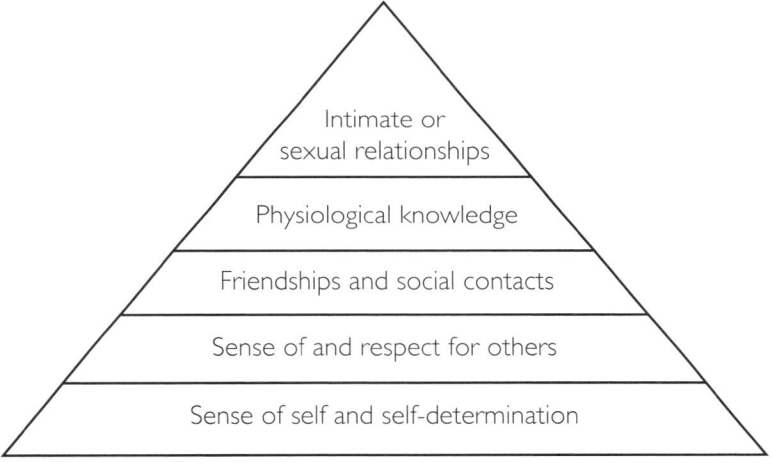

Figure 2 Hierarchy of sexual health learning needs

- The most basic foundations of sexual health learning needs are situated at the base of the pyramid and only when these are achieved should learning blocks from the next layer be taught.
- Sense of self and self-determination includes notions of being a separate entity to the primary carer or parent and the circle of life using mirror work, play and intensive interaction and 'joining' techniques. It also incorporates saying 'no' and being heard.
- Sense of and respect for others involves work on emotions and empathy, public versus private sexual behaviours, naming private body parts, appropriate touch, body space, hygiene and personal safety.
- Friendships and social contacts are largely about social skills, power in relationships, communicating in difficult situations, appropriately communicating emotions and accepting rejection.
- Physiological knowledge examines changes during puberty, sexual intercourse, infections, pregnancy, menstruation, masturbation and sexual health.
- Intimate or sexual relationships can be mutual or solo activities.

Parents will already have beliefs about the role of sex in life, whether this is influenced by religious, cultural or other factors. The following points are generally what are suggested in current literature about sexuality and intellectual disabilities:

- Couch sexual intercourse in the context of loving relationships, which have developed over time and have a balance of power between the partners. Several resources enable parents to discuss this with their children.

- Discuss the range of possible and most common sexual activities. Essentially, these are vaginal, anal and oral sex. Even if parents do not agree with or have never practised some of these, their children might – and need to be safe while doing so (see Resources).

- Give information about contraception and sexually transmitted infections (see below).

For both genders, it is important to warn that a female may bleed slightly when she has her first penetrative vaginal sex, due to the hymen breaking. Parents should remind their daughters that bleeding should happen only once, unless she is having a period. For autistic children this knowledge will prevent anxiety and possible distress if they have sensory issues. Both males and females should know that the man's penis must be erect before it can penetrate the woman's vagina.

THE MENTAL CAPACITY ACT 2005

According to UK current legislation, the capacity to consent to sexual activities is act-specific. UK law uses the rationale that one cannot impose a higher level to a sexual relationship than one uses for marriage in which a sexual component is an integral part. The capacity to consent to sex requires a demonstrable awareness and understanding of the following:

- The mechanics of the sexual act concerned.

- Health risks involved, particularly the possibility of acquiring sexually transmitted infections.

- Sex between a man and a woman can cause the woman to become pregnant.

The Mental Capacity Act 2005 protects the rights of autistic children to make decisions about sexual behaviour. It also imposes an expectation that individuals who do not have capacity to consent should be supported in learning the areas where they have deficits. Present law is designed to ensure that severely autistic people (and people with learning disabilities) have the same rights as other people about issues surrounding sexuality. However, the Learning Disability, Sex and the Law Act 2005 was created to protect individuals with learning disabilities from violence and exploitation.

A case in February 2012 in the UK illustrates the legal minefield involved in notions of capacity to consent. The case witnessed a judge, in effect, banning an autistic woman with an IQ of 64 and mild learning difficulties from having sexual relations (Family Law Week 2012). Mr Justice Hedley found that the woman, H, did not understand the implications of sexual intercourse, so she could not consent to sex. H was placed in local authority housing with one-to-one supervision and was not free to leave her home without this level of supervision, which the judge found to be in the best interests of the woman, given his legal finding that she did not have the capacity to consent to sex (Family Law Week 2012).

The judgment was based on the Mental Capacity Act 2005 but the judge believed that not only was a person required to have knowledge of the physical act of sexual intercourse but also she should have an 'understanding of the moral and emotional components' of what he thought to be a 'complex process' of engaging in sexual acts. However, he acknowledged that there was no reliable test for either of these aspects.

On the basis of H being able to retain information about sexuality, Mr Justice Hedley was not able to conclude lack of capacity to consent. But he found that the woman was unable to translate this knowledge into effective decision-making. Although the judge did not explicitly judge on H's capacity to consent to marriage, this was implicit in his judgment that she could not consent to sexual acts, since these are a key component of marriage and necessary for its consummation.

An important facet of this judgment is that it allowed for improvement in H's condition and development of her levels of maturity, so the order was that her case should be kept under review. Given this judgment, if any person engaged in sexual relations with H even with her express consent, the person could risk conviction for serious sexual assault, because H's consent would be void.

This case was not without precedence. In 2011 the Court of Protection heard the case of a 41-year-old man who had been making lewd and suggestive remarks towards children (Family Law Week 2011). This man had a low IQ and received a similar ban on sexual relations to that of H.

CELIBACY

Celibacy means not having sexual intercourse or sexual relations with another person. Of course, this does not include masturbation or other forms of solo sex. Celibacy is a choice for some non-spectrum people, but may feel less of a choice than a forced situation to someone with more severe end autism. It may help for them to realise that celibacy is a non-spectrum choice or situation.

Some of these children may yearn for a relationship, regardless of how appropriate or likely parents might consider that to be. Many severely autistic people also feel less of a person because of their difference from others in the social world. Aside from facilitating their efforts to create and maintain friendships, parents can reassure their children that many mainstream adults are celibate, sometimes by choice and sometimes because they cannot find a suitable sexual partner.

Even within the context of a relationship some more autistic people choose not to have sexual intercourse. I am aware of several married couples who do not have sex because one or other partner has sensory issues and does not enjoy the 'messiness' of body fluids involved in sex. For others, sex may be highly regimented and timetabled to satisfy their need for routine and rigidity in life.

CONDOM USE

Both males and females should be taught how to put on a condom, to prevent sexually transmitted infections and pregnancy. In non-spectrum young people, they can be taught using an object that might be about the same size as an erect penis, such as a banana or carrot, which are easily accessible at home. For autistic children this teaching method may either distract them, so they lose any meaning behind using the condom, or they may assume that if the condom is on a banana they will be 'safe' having sexual intercourse!

There are several resources available that are shaped like an erect penis, but these young people need to transfer this knowledge of a model into their own sexual practice. Key pieces of information to convey are:

- The male should practise putting on a condom without having a sexual partner present, which can add emotional pressure.

- The penis must be erect to fit on a condom.

- After ejaculation and before the penis becomes flaccid, it should be withdrawn from the partner's orifice, *while holding onto the rim of the condom* to ensure the condom doesn't slip off.

- Water-based lubricant only should be used with condoms.

SEXUALLY TRANSMITTED INFECTIONS

Sexually transmitted infections can be taught in the context of consequences of choices that autistic children might make. Unprotected sex – a choice – can lead to a range of sexually transmitted infections. In males the effects are relatively swift, usually causing one or more of the following symptoms:

- Inflammation (redness) of the end of the penis or anus.

- Weeping fluid (not semen or urine) which may be foul-smelling or green or yellow from the end of the penis or around the anus.

- Itching penis or anus.

- Visible infestation of the pubic hair (with pubic lice, for example).

- Pustules, white blobs (candida) or warts on the penis, particularly the tip.

- Pain on urinating.

In females the symptoms may not be obvious until an infection is well established because much of the sexual organs are internal and invisible. These are the more common symptoms to discuss with or observe for in your daughters:

- Foul-smelling, green or yellow discharge from the vagina.

- White blobs or pustules around the vaginal opening or on the labia (the vaginal lips).

- Itching at the vaginal entrance or labia.

- Visible infestation of the pubic hair.

- Abdominal pain.

- Pain on urinating or having sexual intercourse.

Many of these symptoms can be caused by factors other than sexually transmitted infections. In severely autistic children who still wear nappies or diapers, infections and inflammation may be common, but these children should be seen by a medical practitioner to assess the cause and treatment. Abdominal pain in females is also a notoriously common sign of many different medical conditions in women and would warrant medical investigation.

Treatment for sexually transmitted infections is available free at genitourinary medicine (GUM) clinics or via the family doctor. GUM clinics should be presented to autistic children in a similar way to other practitioners. For example, parents could say that just as opticians help with eye conditions or prescribing spectacles, GUM clinics help with sexual infections. Children who are capable should know what a GUM clinic is and how to contact and locate one. However much parents might like to safeguard their children, those who are able to consent to sex may not want their parents to know if they need to use the services of a GUM clinic. There are several useful resources that parents can use to inform their children (see Resources).

HOMOSEXUALITY AND BISEXUALITY

Homosexuality and bisexuality are emotive areas where religious and moral considerations often play a role. It is thought that bisexuality is common during childhood and preadolescent years, decreasing to around 5 per cent of the population (Masters and Johnson 1988). There has been little research into this aspect of sexuality in autism. One small-scale study found that 35 per cent of autistic residents had a sexual interest in both genders, with 9 per cent being sexually interested in the same sex (Haracopos and Pedersen 1992). There is no reason to suppose that bisexuality or homosexuality is less common in severely autistic people. The emphasis of sexuality teaching should be on providing information to make any sexual contact as safe as it can be without making a judgement about the sexual preference of individuals. Consent to sexual acts is specifically covered in law and, aside from complying with age of consent (16 years in the UK) and restrictions placed on schools to prevent sexual activity on their premises or in public places, there is no legal impediment to someone with severe autism being a practising bisexual or homosexual.

SEX TOYS

Sex toys include a range of devices, such as vibrators, which can enhance sexual experience. High quality products are regarded as 'safe' in terms of any injury they might cause in use and certainly are safe compared with household items which severely autistic children might otherwise use. For some parents sex toys might seem 'seedy' because they have tended to be associated with sex shops, which in turn may be linked to sex workers. Certainly, many parents and caregivers of autistic adolescents will not have so much as visited a sex shop, or even the more socially acceptable high street chain of Ann Summers shops.

The Family Planning Association (FPA), the UK's leading sexual health charity, has developed part of its website to sell sex toys, which it states it carefully selects for quality. This gives parents or autistic children an opportunity to buy products online with plain, discreet packaging for delivery. The 'Desire and Pleasure' section gives advice on cleaning products, safer sex with toys and how to use products and has a broad range of items to purchase.

There are no lasting effects of using sex toys in terms of desensitising genitals; any numbness after use lasts only a few minutes. There is no evidence that using sex toys increases sexual desire, in fact their use may alleviate sexual frustration which might otherwise appear as aggression or depression. Using sex toys is as much 'real' sex as other forms of sexual activity and can be safely enjoyed solo or in a partnership, if both parties consent.

PORNOGRAPHY

The use of pornography is common among the non-spectrum population. It is easily accessed through most newspaper outlets in magazines and is readily available on the internet. For severely autistic people, these avenues may not be so open. Some of them may never enter shops or buy any form of produce without being accompanied. Instead, they may rely on more easily accessible images such as holiday brochures or women's magazines in the home. The argument against providing porn for autistic sons and daughters is that parents may unwittingly promote objectifying others in their children's minds, that is, other people may become mere objects of fantasy. The on-the-fence answer is to allow children to use the porn they can access themselves, but not provide any for their use.

Fantasy plays a significant role in many non-spectrum people's sex lives and parents can speculate that because it is a cognitive activity, it may be less important for severely autistic people. However, it is just as easy to argue that because many people at the severe end of the spectrum have little opportunity to forge actual intimate relationships, they rely more on thinking, even obsessing, about others who arouse them sexually.

Sensory issues in autism may mean that some people on the spectrum may be aroused by objects, such as certain textures or colours, rather than people. This may be as specific as finger nails varnished in scarlet or more broadly, such as toes. Although these may seem odd fascinations, there is little research that describes fantasies of the mainstream population, much of which may seem obscure. My experience as a sexual health counsellor has shown me that fantasies are as numerous as there are people and can involve the most unlikely of subjects. A key difference between mainstream sexual actors and severely autistic ones is that the former are not constantly observed and subject to analysis with few opportunities to enjoy privacy.

Occasionally, a severely autistic person may have a special sexual interest in children and this needs specialist support beyond the realms of this book. Sometimes this can be related to an unwillingness to mature and develop physically, so children become a focus because they have not developed pubic hair and have immature genitals and breasts. This underpins how important it is to educate autistic children about sexual development in a positive, timely and supportive way.

ANXIETY

Anxiety can become pronounced and difficult to manage in adolescence. The most common symptoms are palpitations, profuse perspiring, light-headedness and difficulty breathing, caused by the heart beating faster. All of these are distressing in non-spectrum adolescents who can describe their feelings. How much more alarming for severely autistic children, whose communication skills and ability to understand and locate emotion may be highly limited.

This is when parents' knowledge of their children is important. Other physical signs that parents can look for are an upset gastrointestinal system causing diarrhoea and vomiting, headaches, dry mouth, difficulty in swallowing, trembling and more frequent urination than usual. The psychological effects of irritability, insomnia, heightened sensitivity and fatigue may be displayed by these children as self-injurious behaviours, aggression, new self-stimulatory behaviours (stimming), increased sleep disturbances and new or increased obsessive-compulsive behaviours.

How to Decrease Anxieties

There are several ways to decrease anxieties:

- Using deep pressure massage.

- Having weighted clothing or blankets.

- Using trampolines for regular bouncing or swings for the comforting swinging motion.

- Reviewing the child's diet to exclude possible stimulants such as caffeine, food colourings and excessive sugars.

- Using visual timetabling to ensure your child knows what is going to happen each day.

- Having regular exercise, particularly cardiovascular or aerobic exercise.

These are the basic foundations for sexuality teaching and creating a healthy environment for educating severely autistic children. Chapters 3 and 4 address specific issues for males and females.

CHAPTER 3

BOYS AND MEN

I am starting from the understanding that the goal of parents of autistic boys and men is to enable them to live as independently and socially able as possible for when the parents are no longer capable of supporting them. In terms of sex and sexuality, this goal is underpinned by the knowledge that empowering their children with knowledge and a range of social skills will reduce the likelihood of their children being sexually abused and enhance their ability to create meaningful relationships. Additionally, enabling them to be sexually competent and socially aware will prevent these children unwittingly becoming embroiled in the legal system as sex offenders, with the lasting impact that might have on their lives.

Changing established behaviours can be onerous and prolonged, especially in autistic people who thrive on set routines. Unwanted sexual behaviours, such as public masturbation or frottage (body-rubbing), can take months to eradicate and may only be reduced to a manageable level. It is always better to start educating before any sexual issues occur.

PHYSICAL CHANGES

Boys start to produce the hormone testosterone at around the age of ten years and physical changes are unlikely to be seen before that age. It is important that parents start preparing their sons for these alterations well in advance, possibly by noting the difference between sons and their fathers physically, depending on your house rules around nakedness. Certainly, picture books such as the *Books Beyond Words* series show clear pictures of the maturing male body (see Resources).

It is critical that boys understand the following:

- These physical changes do not take place overnight. Boys will start by noticing one or two underarm or scrotal hairs which slowly increase in number, and are part of ordinary maturing into an adult.

- In future other physical changes slowly take place, such as greying pubic hair.

- This is a positive thing and the parents' love for their sons will not change with their appearance.

- All other boys (including those who are not different or have autism) change in a similar way as they get older.

Ways of Conveying Gradual and Slow Changes

Here are some ways of helping boys understand gradual changes:

- Look at nature, perhaps plants growing either indoors or outdoors which may be helpful.

- If parents buy a young animal, they can work with their sons to show how the animal develops over time into a stronger, larger creature, which is still the same animal, just different and still loved as much.

- Magazines, newspapers or comics may yield pictures to help parents explain the meaning of gradual change too.

- Internet programmes showing boys growing older, into young men, older men then ageing men, will reinforce the notion of constant change as being a 'given'.

Parents should check their sons' understanding of any concepts they are trying to teach and remember to repeat the information. This is likely to be opportunistically with this notion of slow development – parents may think of something they see regularly that is slowly developing. Many autistic children, even those with greater communication skills, find the concept of their bodies changing alarming and something they want to stop if possible. My own son spent some time telling me that 'Jude little boy, no big boy' when we started working on these changes. Although his body hasn't started changing physically, I often refer to him as my 'lovely big boy' and he now realises that he is bigger and some of his school peers are still 'little' but will grow over time.

Other Concepts around Preparation

Demonstrate the differences between fluids, so that boys can physically feel the difference between watery fluids and sticky, less runny fluids. This helps when parents explain about urine and semen both being produced from the penis, but having different qualities. Whatever fluids parents use to help explain this, they should remember when talking about wet dreams or erections, to tell their sons this is not what actually comes out of their penises; it is just *like* what comes out. The internet can be useful for showing precisely what happens at the point of ejaculation, although many sites are pornographic (see Resources for suitable products).

Illustrate the differences between hard and soft, using objects to show boys and helping them feel which are more solid or more flexible, for example. Again this helps when explaining about erections, when the less runny, milky coloured fluid comes out of the penis, and the flaccid (floppy) penis when they are able to urinate. Parents should make sure that boys understand that they cannot produce urine from an erect penis and that they realise that their penises may become hard but will return to being soft and vice versa. One sad example is a severely autistic young man who was scared that his penis would snap or break when it was hard, so he was terrified of it becoming erect. For some parents who find sexuality a problem, this might seem like a solution. For the young man, he was constantly anxious, to the point where he started self-mutilating behaviours and became aggressive.

From the earliest point of giving their sons baths as very young children, parents can introduce the idea of being clean or washing away dirt. This is important for the future when they come to discuss hygiene as their sons produce more hormones and need to keep fresh, and when they need to clean themselves after masturbation. Teaching their sons to clean and take care of their own private parts will prevent the boys relying on others, which is one aspect of preventing sexual abuse. Washing under the foreskin with gentle soap is vital to prevent smegma building up, which smells offensive and can lead to inflammation or infection on the glans penis. The penis naturally produces lubricant which, if not cleaned by gently easing back the foreskin, will accumulate. The foreskin remains attached to the length of the penis until about the age of ten years onwards, so you should not try to draw it back before this. If a boy has started to masturbate, the foreskin is more than likely able to retract.

Bathing is also an opportunity to encourage boys to smell the difference between clean and dirty things. Generally helping them to use their sense of smell will acclimatise them to the concept, which they will need as they mature to detect body odour or halitosis and ensure they stay clean. This may sound superficial, but parents want their sons to socialise as much as possible to develop skills and be included in society; if boys are unwashed and odorous, any avenues for socialising may close. This is where preparation around others' feelings is an important basic piece of learning, because they won't bother washing if they have no concept of others. Clearly this is even more important if they are to develop any meaningful friendships or intimate relationships.

Again bathing gives the opportunity for parents to explore with their sons from an early age or understanding, the meaning of 'wet' versus 'dry' or levels of these in between. This is helpful when they reach puberty because they can explain or simply understand that some fluids cause things to be wet or damp and how to return the object, such as bed sheets or pyjamas, to a state of dryness when they will be comfortable for the next night's sleep. This is particularly important when dealing with wet dreams.

Two footnotes to independent washing are first be aware that some autistic children develop obsessive compulsive tendencies, meaning that they will repeatedly perform certain tasks, such as washing themselves, to the point where the behaviour takes over their existence. Encouraging washing should place that activity in the context of being dirty or a routine before bed, for example, rather than 'practising' repeatedly with boys so that they perfect the behaviour. Second, some autistic children have 'pica', which is the obsessive impulse to eat objects, regardless of whether or not they are food or drink. Sometimes pica is caused by lack of zinc but it may be a feature of boys which cannot be modified so parents have to account for it in everything they do with their sons. In washing, this may mean taking care over what soaps or cloths they use, never using sponges or liquid soaps or shower gels, so that they encourage their sons' independence while minimising potential harm to them.

Feeling themselves and knowing how they feel and what is 'normal' for them is important, so boys recognise changes that may not be part of ordinary physical development and can draw parents' or caregivers' attention to this. For example, regularly feeling their testicles will allow lumps, such as malignancies, to be identified readily by men. Another aspect of maturing is poor skin, caused by hormones during puberty. Encouraging boys from an early point in childhood to observe themselves in the mirror or look at their own bodies will help them to recognise changes.

Encourage boys to draw their parents' attention to any illness they have and identify where in their bodies they feel unwell, as well as what type of illness they feel. Again this can be started at as early an age as they can communicate and work with school to use the same symbols or pictures. Using a diagram, parents can train their sons to point to or mark on a picture the location of the 'ill' part, then give them choices and enable them to identify how that part is ill. For instance, are they having a 'stabbing' or 'throbbing' pain or 'dull ache' which can be related to colours or numbers, depending on the child's abilities? Do they feel nauseas or want to vomit?

BODY PARTS

Severely autistic children need to be able to identify parts of their body for many reasons:

- helping to locate illness

- recognising when something is wrong with their body, even if it is painless, such as tumours

- understanding if sexual abuse has happened

- helping to describe sexual abuse

- developing intimate relationships.

In terms of sexuality and sexual health the following areas involve crucial changes to the body which need explaining in the context of naming body parts:

- skin

- voice

- hair

- shaving

- the penis

- testicles.

Skin

Skin, often the face, can erupt in pustules or spots and can be painful and therefore alarming to young men, if they have no explanation of what is happening. My son developed one spot on his nose, which absorbed his whole existence until it naturally burst and the skin recovered. No amount of encouragement would persuade him to let me even touch it, although it was clearly painful.

The skin of the penis and testicles changes from wrinkled to being taut during sexual arousal, which may appear alarming to young autistic boys. The colour of the glans can change to purplish-red as well. If identified for young men prior to a point where they might have erections, they are prepared and will be less anxious. A drawing or picture may be helpful, although the size of an erect penis might be scary, so find one without scale (see Resources).

Voice

Parents should not tell their sons that their voices will 'break' and ensure that all others involved in their support don't, either. Saying that their voices will become lower as they slowly become grown men and that it won't hurt and won't ever go back to being a child's higher voice are important to convey.

Hair

Use a drawing to explain that pubic hairs will grow on young men's penises and testicles as well as underarm, chest and facial hair as they grow up. Parents should remember to tell young men that only one or two hairs will grow to start with and only over time will others grow. Some of the available pictures about puberty appear to suggest that a mat of hairs forms quickly on each zone and this could frighten children.

Pubic hairs are itchy when they grow, so boys need to know this. If young men are incontinent, it may be more hygienic to carefully clip the pubic hairs, which otherwise make cleaning more difficult and the hairs retain odours.

Shaving

With growth of facial hair comes the need to shave, largely because facial hair can be itchy. Many autistic people have sensory issues so young men may opt to shave. They will also observe that most men in western cultures are clean shaven or have sculpted beards and/or moustaches. It can take months to acclimatise young men to the feeling and sounds of an electric razor. Often the best approach is to allow autistic children to feel the buzzing sensation on their hands, before their faces. If parents leave the cover over the shaver, they will avoid blunders and alarming their child with an extra sensation too soon. It is wise to take the cover off when their sons are used to the feeling of the vibration. The timing of all this depends on how individual children manage. It is helpful if children have experienced having their hair shaved, even if this is just to edge the hairline. So it may be worthwhile introducing this early in their hairdressing repertoire.

This underpins the need to encourage autistic children to expand their social experiences, which can be built on during adolescence and beyond. One mother recently told me how her son hated the hairdresser so much when he was very young that he would scream and become highly distressed. This is common. Her response was to curtail all future hairdressing for him. At the point when I was discussing this with her, the now young man of 19 years of age was having his hair cut regularly by his mother at home, which had been the situation since he was five years old. She confirmed she shaved his face with a razor because he could not stand the vibration of an electric shaver, but she had not persisted in persuading him to attend the barbers. What this mother failed to see is that she was creating dependence and preventing a socially interactive and developmental opportunity for him in getting out to the barbers, which is a haven for interacting with other men and observing non-spectrum male behaviours.

My ten-year-old autistic son adores the barbers, although it took several months of sitting in the shop watching, then sitting in the booster chair before he finally agreed to let the barber touch his hair with scissors, slowly introducing and building up to a shaver being used to edge his hair. Especially because I am sole parent to both my children, this is a great chance for my son to mingle with testosterone and learn by observation.

If a young man wants to manage a razor or has a poor response to an electric shaver, parents should take the process in stages again. If there is another male in the home who shaves, he can demonstrate how to do it. It is wise to keep the shield over the blade initially, so that boys can practise without risking multiple cuts. There is a skill to shaving with a razor, involving coordinating hand and facial movements, so parents may need to shave their sons' faces while they learn how to manoeuvre their jaw to aid shaving. Practise hand-over-hand, then finally boys may shave independently. This may take months to achieve.

Shaving as a process can also enable young men to groom themselves and take some pride in their appearance, which is a vital part of self-esteem. It is important that parents invest the time to enable their sons to be independent shavers.

The Penis

Young men will be well acquainted with their penises from urinating and washing. They may have started to feel sensations associated with sex even if they have not started masturbating yet. It is critical that they understand that their penises may become hard sometimes and may seep sticky, not-so-runny fluid into their underpants. They may wish to touch their penises and they may respond to unusual triggers which stimulate erections.

Without support and clear education, severely autistic children may imagine things can occur which are impossible but which would totally undermine any hope of satisfactory sexual activity, either solo or with a partner. For example, in one piece of research a severely autistic man stated that when he ejaculated his mind was overtaken with images of thousands of babies who would not be born and another was terrified of the fantasies that accompanied his masturbation.

Testicles

It is better to use the correct names, rather than pet names, so that males can report any illness or other issues. Pubic hair and changes to the size of their testicles can make boys feel uncomfortable. Useful resources are listed at the end of this book, which parents can work through with their sons, which use pictures and suggest exercises to do.

WET DREAMS OR NOCTURNAL EMISSIONS

In the process of puberty boys will wake, often having ejaculated in their sleep. Without an explanation or understanding, this can be frightening for severely autistic boys. The irony of nocturnal emissions in severe autism is that they occur just at the point when some young men have started to manage nocturnal urination.

The fluid may make them think they have urinated in their sleep and might get into trouble with their parents. In one case, this was so severe a fear that the young man would not go to sleep and became aggressive and distressed. This is when it is important that they recognise the difference between the yellow fluid of urine and the white, slightly sticky and less runny fluid of semen. Parents should couch what is happening to them in terms of a gradual process of growing up and something that is acceptable and that happens to all boys. Parents can reassure them that they will stop having these periods of waking soaked and will have them only occasionally after they have grown into 'men'. It is important that they realise wet dreams can occur even when they are fully matured, so that they are not alarmed.

Young men should be encouraged to tell parents when they have had a wet dream so they can put on clean sheets or, if they are able encourage sons to remove their sheets and/or help change the bed as part of being responsible for themselves. This will enable them better to manage as they become more independent. There are good resources parents can work through with their sons.

UNWANTED SPONTANEOUS ERECTIONS

Many people with autism have sensory issues, which can mean they enjoy what might seem to non-spectrum individuals to be bizarre sensory experiences, while having difficulties with what otherwise seem unchallenging. Things that usually stimulate a sexual response in a male might be photographs of people in bathing costumes or people exercising. Less obvious triggers might be metal containers, toes or gold threads running through fabric.

Seemingly 'odd' objects that sexually arouse severely autistic sons may cause consternation and distress to parents, who may suddenly be presented with their sons having an erection in a public place with no apparent cause. Unlike non-spectrum men, who would use a policy of thinking about something non-sexual to reduce an unwanted erection, this would not work with autistic sons because of their lack of imagination and ability to self-distract. Parents could try:

- physically removing their sons from a situation
- physically covering the erection if possible until they are distracted or the erection has passed
- giving them something physical to do
- giving them a sensory object
- ensuring they have masturbation timetabled into their day (see below).

One of the most effective ways of dealing with this issue is to locate the source of arousal, bearing in mind it might be obscure and parents might have to undergo several potentially embarrassing experiences in the process. Once parents have located the stimulus, they can create books for their sons, loaded with images they enjoy of the source of arousal. Parents can develop the books with sons by using pictures from magazines and newspapers which they indicate arouse them. Without their input the exercise may be fruitless because parents cannot instinctively know what turns on their sons sexually.

Parents can name the book as simply the 'Foot Book', for example, and store it for their sons to use when masturbating, removing it when it is not in use. They can refer to this when their sons become aroused in public, stating that they can have the Foot Book when they return home. If it is already used regularly with masturbation, unwanted erections are likely to be fewer and may be reduced by the promise of the book, removal from the situation and/or a sensory object.

PARAPHILIAS

Paraphilias are categorised as 'deviance' but are very often explicable in severely autistic males. They may include stealing underwear, wearing or using others' underwear for arousal, or using objects such as taps or vacuum cleaner hoses anally to accelerate ejaculation. These often are related to childhood sexual experiences and are ritualistic sexual behaviours which autistic people find necessary to achieve arousal and reach climax.

Sometimes severely autistic males may behave in a way that seems to be paraphilias, such as using urinals with their underpants down or unzipping jeans before entering the lavatory. In fact, these actions are explained by a lack of sex education and knowledge of social norms around the use of public lavatories.

MEDICATION AND SEXUAL ACTIVITY

I would be reluctant to suggest any medication unless absolutely essential for any severely autistic children, particularly those who are younger than their early twenties, when the brain is still growing and developing. However, antipsychotic drugs are prescribed to alleviate aggressive or self-injurious behaviours and these can cause suppression of a person's libido, with difficulty gaining an erection and reaching climax (Mitchell and Popkin 1983).

There is insufficient evidence about the long-term effects of medication specifically taken to reduce sexual activity. One of the known side-effects of these drugs is the growth of breasts in men (gynaecomastia). Behavioural approaches have shown positive results, even if it is a reduction rather than complete resolution to cited problems.

In extreme cases, when educational and behavioural approaches have been exhausted, there may be an argument for an antiandrogen, such as Leuprolide, which can be injected. The dose can be titrated until it is effective but as low as it can be (Realmuto and Ruble 1999).

PAYING FOR SEXUAL ACTIVITY

Sometimes parents have paid for sex workers to give their disabled sons sexual pleasure. Whatever parents' moral judgements (or not) about this, there are a couple of points worth noting if parents consider this an option:

- Their sons may believe that any woman is available for this service (or vice versa), especially as autistic people find it tricky to understand that different rules apply to different situations or people.

- Their sons may become embroiled in the legal system if they try to pay for sex where it is illegal, or if they start to kerb-crawl to find a woman, or if they get aggressive if a woman refuses to have sex with them for money, for example.

- This activity would encourage a negative approach from their sons towards women in general since they have paid for a sexual service or vice versa. Although they might gain hugely in self-esteem, the situation is false and cannot be transposed into their ordinary lives.

Some people may argue that paying for sex may increase young men's risk of sexually transmitted infections. I would argue the opposite; my experience of working with sex workers is that they have a keen awareness of such infections, particularly HIV, and are proponents of using condoms.

The most legitimate argument I would make is that there is no evidence to show that this experience would have a lasting positive effect on young men. It may actually worsen the situation because they may be more frustrated that they are not in a relationship, which may be the goal of many of them despite their lack of opportunity and skills.

The law states that parents and caregivers should not promote or facilitate sexual opportunities in which their children cannot make informed choices. Paying for sex undermines much of the work that parents do with autistic children around sexuality, where they support their children in not accepting gifts, money or other favours in return for sex. If parents are paying for sex workers, they open their children up to sexual exploitation.

The only time some intellectually disabled people feel 'normal' is when they have sexual intercourse. Other than this, they are not allowed to drive or permitted to go freely wherever they want without being constantly observed, and they are often treated like children. This can be the case regardless of IQ or verbal communication skills.

USING PUBLIC LAVATORIES

One of the most important lessons that males can learn about public behaviours is what to do – and not do – in public lavatories. What they are allowed to do in the privacy of the bathroom at home is simply not social etiquette in the public arena. Men could land themselves in trouble with the police or simply be attacked by a fellow lavatory user if, for example, they stare at or comment on another man's penis at the urinals.

Having a trusted adult male (such as the child's father) accompany sons into public lavatories can certainly enable them to practise proper behaviours. However, I would suggest using a story or draw what is expected *before* entering public lavatories; rehearsing or role-playing the scenario will help it go smoothly first time. If there are immediate problems, males may perceive public lavatories as scary places.

Rules of Public Lavatories for Men
URINALS

- Urinals are only for urinating in.

- Avoid eye contact: it may seem easy for someone with autism to avoid eye contact, but this will probably be the one occasion when sons decide to make the eye contact parents so long for and encourage.

- Don't stand next to another person using a urinal – try to find the furthest urinal from anyone else.

- Only unzip trousers to access the penis – do not take down trousers and underpants.

- Don't look around when using the urinal – scan up and down or look straight ahead.

CUBICLES

- Cubicles ('stalls' to US readers) may be used for urinating or defecating, but usually men use urinals if they want to urinate.

- Do not remove any clothing or unzip trousers before entering the cubicle.

- Lock the door behind them and do not unlock until they are fully dressed and zipped.

- Do not comment on noises they hear from other cubicles or urinals.

- Take their wallets and other possessions into the cubicle with them.

- Wash hands and leave the lavatory building without engaging in conversation with others – again, this is the opposite to the social communication parents usually encourage in their sons, so identify for their children that this is different in public lavatories.

Although parents may think their sons are too severely autistic to ever use a public lavatory alone, there are some scenarios which may cause this to happen. For example:

- Males want to use the lavatory when they are out with a female. This is particularly pertinent for single mothers, like me.

- Males are out as part of a larger group with paid caregivers and one individual wants to use the lavatory. Despite adhering to rules around caregiver to client ratios, sons may need to use the lavatory alone while the rest of the group waits outside for them.

- Males are with a group being supported by only female caregivers, who make up around 80–95 per cent of paid caregivers so they have to use public lavatories alone (McConkey *et al.* 2007).

CHAPTER 4

GIRLS AND WOMEN

The overall goal of parents of autistic girls or women should be to enhance their abilities to live independently, as far as is possible. Historically, females have been viewed as weaker and more vulnerable than males and this perspective is often amplified when considering those with severe autism. The temptation is to protect autistic daughters by cosseting them and building social and physical barriers around them to prevent their being injured either physically or emotionally. While parents are still alive, this may seem constructive. However, to truly support autistic daughters, parents need to cater for the worst possible future scenario when they are no longer here.

Empowering severely autistic girls and women with sexual knowledge, opportunities to experience friendships and enhancing as far as possible communication and social skills will reduce their likelihood of becoming sexually exploited or abused. Regardless of what parents might expect, their severely autistic daughters will menstruate and will have sexual desires. They will become physically strong and want to act on sexual feelings. If they do not receive sexuality education – and early – this could create an environment where they act inappropriately in public places or with strangers. Ultimately, this might cause their involvement with the legal and judicial system and/or severe limitations to their integration into any community. The aim of this chapter is to address these issues.

BODY PARTS

Parents need to prepare their daughters for physical changes that will naturally occur as they mature. This needs to be conveyed as a gradual process, not a sudden alteration to their appearance. Additionally, helping their daughters understand that all women grow up in the same way may encourage them to embrace the changes, because many severely autistic people yearn to be like non-spectrum others. Fear of maturing is associated with eating disorders in girls on the autism spectrum, since lack of nutrition prevents breasts developing and periods starting.

In terms of sexual health, the following areas involve crucial changes to the body:

- spots

- hair

- shaving

- breasts

- hips

- vagina

- moods

- libido.

Spots

Simple though this may seem, it is important to mention that facial blemishes particularly will happen and that this is normal and will improve or go away eventually. Spots can be painful and alarming to severely autistic females, causing concern that they are 'ill', or they simply become distressed. Dealing with spots using particular facial washes or creams is something that can be introduced before their faces erupt with spots in puberty. Parents can help their daughters practise washing their faces carefully around their eyes, for example, so that when they need to use an ointment, they already know to take care.

Hair

Autistic girls need to be warned about pubic hair, that it will appear in armpits as well as in the crotch. They need to understand that only one or two hairs will grow initially, then gradually more until they are unable to count them, but they won't become hairy like an ape. They should understand that, although they might want to copy advertisements or women on movies and shave their hairs, the hairs over their vagina are not shaven; legs and armpits are the areas to shave.

Pubic hair can be itchy as it grows, so girls should be warned that this is to be expected. If young women are not continent it may be wise, if possible, to carefully trim the pubic hair to stop it retaining odours and making hygiene more difficult to maintain.

Shaving

Shaving anything will be difficult initially. Although a relatively small area, the armpits are tricky because they can be seen only via a mirror and involve holding the arm in a particular way to expose the part that needs shaving. In many ways, the legs are easier for young women to practise on because they are larger areas and more visible without having to use a mirror. It may feel less onerous to persuade daughters to shave only their armpits which may be more obvious in public, but legs may be better for practice and they may eventually progress to shaving them, anyway. Or they may decide never to shave anything!

If parents plump for electric razors, they may need to help their daughters desensitise by having them feel the razor as it buzzes, so they can get used to the sensation and sounds. Then put it to their skin over time to adjust to the feeling before any actual shaving can be done. Parents need to remember to show them how to clean out the razor, which is likely to fill quickly if they are tackling legs and armpits. Parents should take their daughters with them to choose an electric razor, or if this is difficult due to sensory or other issues, use a catalogue or online service to choose.

If parents opt for a traditional 'wet' razor, it is wise to practise the movements using shaving gel or foam and a razor with the cover left on. Once their daughters are comfortable with handling what can feel like a thin handle, parents can take the cover off but use a large area such as the calves for practice. The usual rules about repetition apply; parents may need to repeat the basic information and practise with the cover on before finally using the razor with the blade exposed many times before starting directly to use the uncovered razor.

Waxing is a possibility. It lasts for two to three weeks, much longer than shaving, but is painful. Hair removal creams are messy and toxic and would present the opportunity for a range of traumas. Many severely autistic children appreciate that they are different and want to do regular grooming activities, such as shaving. Parents can get their daughter involved in purchasing and learning how to shave.

Dark haired females may need to learn how to shave facial hair above the upper lip. Certainly, most women have to remove hairs from chins and cheeks in their 50-plus years. Plucking, waxing or even hydrolysis would be the option for most non-spectrum women but, again, these are painful methods, so shaving may be the best choice.

Autistic females need to see the issue of hair as part of the cycle of life, of transitioning in puberty into adults, then developing into older people when they will become more hairy due to lack of hormones.

Breasts

As they grow and develop, girls' breasts can be sensitive. Sometimes even brushing past something can cause pain, so it is important for parents to forewarn their daughters. Breast size can vary and breasts will continue to grow during puberty. Severely autistic girls need to understand that breast growth is, again, a gradual process and that breasts may swell slightly before having a period, too.

A good exercise is for parents to take their daughters to have their breast size measured at a shop and choose a bra. This teaches their daughters several things:

- Breasts are different sizes and shapes for everyone.

- Only special shop 'bra experts' should be measuring their breasts.

- A well-fitted bra will prevent backache or general discomfort in the breasts.

- Girls can take pride in their appearance and experience taking care of themselves, which encourages a level of self-esteem and responsibility.

Even if severely autistic young women do not appear able to communicate at a level where parents feel they can benefit from this exercise, it is worthwhile ensuring they have well-fitted bras, as parents would with any other piece of clothing. Parents should remember to replace bras over time.

Teaching their daughters how to put on a bra independently is an important part of parents' creating independence, especially as the bra covers an intimate part of the body. Parents need to feel that their children will not have to ask for help with private tasks if at all possible. One of the easiest ways to put on a bra is to have a front-fastening bra, but this may limit the range to choose from. Alternatively, the young woman can pull the back fastener to the front, do it up, then twist the whole bra so that the cups are at the front and the fastener at the back. Then she can lean forwards and 'catch' her breasts in each cup and put her arms through the shoulder straps. This will take some time to learn, but, once learnt, the daily routine will ensure that the young woman knows exactly how to put on a bra without help.

Hips

Not only do a girl's breasts develop but also her hips and buttocks will become larger and more rounded in preparation for motherhood (childbearing hips). This would frighten girls if they had no understanding of this and may become the root of not eating if the child has sufficient insight or can make a connection.

Vagina

In sexuality education, the term 'vagina' tends to be used as a generic term for what is medically the vagina (the orifice and channel to the cervix at the end of the uterus), the labia (the external lips) and the clitoris (the sensitive blob of flesh near the vaginal opening).

Severely autistic girls and women need to be aware that fluid will seep from the vagina and may appear on their underwear. The fluid may feel tickly and then damp, both of which can feel uncomfortable to autistic people, who have sensory issues. Some girls and women may feel more content to wear thin pads all the time which can be changed if they feel dampness. The colour and smell of any fluid leaked is important for girls and women to acknowledge, so they can report if either of these change, which may indicate infection.

Moods

Parents should guide their children to understand the range of emotions they may experience but must also anticipate these, so parents do not assume their autism is worsening when their children start to demonstrate anger or distress, for example. Daughters may feel anger, upset, tiredness, frustration or tearfulness due to fluctuations in hormone levels. Helping them recognise that this is to be expected is critical. Even non-spectrum teenagers can feel overwhelmed by powerful emotions so parents can expect their autistic children to feel the same, but with less insight, unless parents anticipate this for them.

Libido

Having a different body shape, larger breasts and surges of hormones can all promote greater libido (sexual desire) in daughters. Without guidance, they may be sexual with others, act inappropriately in public or be susceptible to abuse. Of course, another scenario is that young women may forge a relationship with another person, which is physical and consenting. Becoming sexually mature can be a positive experience.

MENSTRUATION

Periods start on average in the UK at 12 years of age, with some girls starting as young as eight years old, regardless of any learning difficulties or severe autism. If parents are to prepare their daughters adequately for this transition into adulthood, they need to start the process early. Menstruation links together several strands of basic learning around sexuality; concepts of 'dirty' and 'clean', issues around what is 'public' and 'private' as well as self-awareness and physical development. In a very real sense, the menstrual cycle demonstrates the absolute importance of teaching the cornerstones of sex education early and often as a means of preparing autistic daughters for this fundamental long-term change.

Daughters need to know that, whether or not they are going to be mothers at any point in their lives, their bodies will prepare as if they will be. Each month a woman's body produces a tiny egg which, if it joins with sperm in the woman's body, will develop into a foetus or baby. Young women should understand that sperm comes from the man or boy's penis and is in the sticky, not so runny fluid he produces.

The woman's womb or uterus prepares for a possible foetus by building up a spongy wall for the foetus to embed in. If the egg and sperm do not meet and join in the woman, the spongy stuff is shed and comes out of the vagina as blood. This is not the same as an injury ('ouch' or 'hurt' or whatever word the family uses) but just happens every month in all women. However, parents must explain that their daughters may ache or have abdominal cramps during a period. Before their daughter starts menstruating, parents should use a pain chart to enable their children to locate pain and explain the type of pain for anything from headaches to a sprained ankle. If these children are able to visually demonstrate pain before having a period, it will help because young women will have additional issues to deal with in having periods, such as feeling emotional, dizzy or scared seeing blood.

Some autistic daughters will not be able to tell or show parents that they have cramps or pains associated with menstruating. Parents need to be aware that these young women may show pain by behaving differently, perhaps aggressively or by self-inflicted injuries such as biting or scratching their limbs. They may also feel their crotch or lower abdomen, which may be confused with attempts to masturbate, especially as this behaviour can induce immediate and emotive responses in parents. In cases where behaviour change is indicative of pain or may presumptively be, it is a good idea to give analgesia (pain relief) regularly through a period in anticipation and to prevent distress. Over the counter medication, such as ibuprofen or paracetamol, should suffice but check with the pharmacist that there are no interactions with any medicine the young women are prescribed or taking already. Warm hot water bottles and warm baths can help relieve discomfort as well.

Eventually, when their daughters are much older, they will stop having the bleeding because their bodies cannot have children any longer. Parents can make the connection between the cycle of life (getting old) and stopping the menstrual cycle at 45–55 years of age.

Managing Periods

As with most issues for autistic people, forewarning and preparation are critical. Most learning is best achieved through visual methods, but using opportunities to facilitate learning through other senses can be effective. For example, using a liquid that appears to be the colour of blood, such as water with food colouring in, will be a way of girls feeling as well as seeing what to expect during a period. You can show how the fluid sinks into a sanitary pad (be wary of using the term sanitary 'towel' as this can be confused with drying towels).

Sensory issues can be difficult to anticipate, such as dislike of the smell of menstrual blood. If mothers feel able to do so, showing their daughters their own menstrual blood on a sanitary pad will give them the best idea of the smell and sight of blood. A concern they may have is how much blood they will produce, or how quickly they will lose blood if it gushes or trickles out. In reality only an average 30–40 ml of blood is lost in the totality of a period, so parents can show how little this is and that this is not a daily amount, but trickles out over several days.

Another important point to make is that the colour and amount of blood alters as the period progresses. So there may be very little, pinkish blood initially, which becomes more in quantity and red in colour, then finally becomes brownish and very little as a period ends. These details are important to prevent girls becoming distressed when what appears on their sanitary pad is not what they expected. Blood, of course, is usually associated with being ill or injured in the body and the sight of it can panic some individuals. The other significant point is that detailed information ensures that young women are aware when something is unusual, which should be reported, such as excessive blood loss, which could indicate a medical condition called menorrhagia.

Before severely autistic girls start their periods, parents can practise helping their children stick a sanitary pad into pants then pull the pants up without the pressure of actual blood, emotion, dizziness or pain. Usually light-coloured underwear will enable young women to readily see if they have leaked blood and change their pads, even if this is not at a time on their visual schedules. Parents can use a marker pen to indelibly mark on pants where the sanitary pad should be stuck. If using a 'winged' sanitary pad, remember to wrap the wings around the gusset before pulling up the underwear, otherwise there is a likelihood of pubic hair being caught on the adhesive and hurting. Repetition and practice will enable severely autistic young women and reassure them.

For some females, tampons are an option. This may not immediately seem appropriate for a severely autistic child, but remember that these children continue to develop socially and in communication skills, so tampons may be something to discuss at a future point. If mothers do not use tampons, or a father is helping with menstruation, parents should try not to let this discourage them from seeing this as a viable choice for young women. Tampons can make women feel cleaner and have fewer blood-staining accidents with their underwear, both of which can be distressing to autistic females. If girls can masturbate using their fingers to massage their vaginas, they may learn the skills to insert and remove tampons.

Practise with a variety of sizes of tampons, with and without applicators and coloured water. Parents should let their daughters feel the difference in the tampons, see how the applicator works and see that tampons swell as they become damp. Remember that the applicator is precisely that; it does not remain inside the woman. A female friend, using her first tampon as a teenager, left the applicator in her vagina and had to get her mother to remove it – and she is not autistic.

Parents should have their daughters practise wrapping up damp, used sanitary pads and tampons in toilet tissue or a small bag (like the ones provided in public lavatories) and place them in a bin. Parents should show their daughters the sanitary containers in public lavatories and how to open them to insert the bag containing the used tampon or sanitary pad.

Resources are available which contain symbols and pictures on cards to help parents explain about sanitary pads and tampons (see Resources).

While young women are learning to manage their periods, they should be encouraged to wear dark underwear and trousers in case of accidental leaks, although parents may feel that seeing the leaks may be a visual cue to remind their daughters to change their sanitary pads more often. However, I would argue that seeing the blood and creating spoiled underwear and clothing may be more distressing. A way of prompting young women to change their sanitary wear is not to rely on them feeling damp or seeing leaks, but to give them regular times throughout their day to change them, such as every break at school, after each meal and before they go to bed. This can be done using a visual timetable. Some severely autistic girls may respond well to a reward system for managing their personal hygiene and periods.

If young women are unable to physically or mentally manage their periods, it is still important to introduce them to the 'paraphernalia' of sanitary pads and the fact that they will bleed, like other women. Again, parents cannot predict how well their children will socially develop, so even some of the most severely autistic girls will develop skills to manage at least some aspects of menstruation.

Parents should reinforce the need for careful hand-washing, which is part of basic teaching of hygiene and should be established by the time girls start menstruating. Once menstruation has begun, plotting periods visually on a calendar can help autistic girls and parents anticipate any accompanying issues, such as initiating analgesia for pain a day or two before a period is due. Periods happen on average every 28 days, but may be anywhere from 24 to 35 days, sometimes being irregular initially, but getting more regular as they become established.

Hygiene

Hormones, pubic hair wet with urine and various discharges from the vagina and menstruation make hygiene critically important. When teaching girls about self-care, parents should tell them to wash 'front to back', from the vaginal area to the anal area. The anus has more potential for infection due to bacteria which are naturally in the bowel. Since it is the 'dirtier' zone, it should be washed last to prevent bacteria being swept forward and causing infection in the vagina.

It is helpful if parents introduce deodorants, fragranced soaps or other perfumed toiletries and invite their daughters to participate in choosing them. This is all part of developing self-esteem and being self-determined and should create a greater likelihood that they will attend to personal hygiene. It should be a priority to make severely autistic females as independent as possible in washing and hygiene for their own self-esteem and to minimise the possibility of sexual abuse.

WHAT IS SEXUAL INTERCOURSE?

The mechanics of sex may seem less important than the relationship to parents, who may hope that keeping their children ignorant of sex will prevent them becoming sexually active. It will simply leave them open to abuse. Giving precise information about sexual intercourse will:

- ensure that women know what they are consenting to if they have a relationship and agree to have sex with a partner

- help them to understand how contraception works, particularly condoms which are proven to prevent sexually transmitted infections

- help them prevent pregnancy
- help them recognise sexual abuse
- help them accurately report sexual abuse.

PREGNANCY

Whatever parents' thoughts about their autistic daughters having children, they cannot dictate their daughters' desires to have babies. This is a very basic instinct in humanity and a way in which many of our daughters will feel 'normal' if they can achieve it. Clearly even having friendships, leave alone sexual relationships, is beyond the capacity of some of the most severely autistic daughters. However, I would caution again about keeping expectations flexible because parents cannot project how much their children will socially develop throughout their lives. As stated earlier, autistic children have sexual rights which may override the personal feelings of parents about their intimate lives. Of all severely autistic children in the UK, only about 300–400 need to be in institutions according to recent reports following the Winterbourne View inquiry (Borland 2012; Department of Health 2013), so these are the least likely to have any ability to form consensual sexual relationships.

CONTRACEPTION

Contraception can only be taught once young women have a grasp of physical changes and the mechanics of sexual intercourse. Condoms may be the only means of preventing sexually transmitted infections, but other contraception may be worth examining to prevent the possibility of unwanted pregnancy. There are many more routes of contraception nowadays, and parents may be completely unaware of the advances that have taken place.

Parents need to encourage their autistic daughters to include family planning or GUM clinics as part of their social world. Parents should place these alongside dentists for tooth care and family planning for sexual health care. Enabling their daughters to access these clinics, to visit with them and give them all contact details, will ensure their girls use these facilities as they need to in their future lives, even if this involves taking a sexual partner rather than parents with them for a consultation.

Family planning clinics can advise on the most appropriate form of contraception for women, taking into account their likelihood of remembering to take the contraceptive pill, for example. Contraception for females includes tablets, patches, implants, injections or devices placed in the uterus and their use should be monitored medically.

Sterilisation and Termination of Pregnancy

Historically sterilisation was used to prevent pregnancies in what were perceived to be people who should not have children. Not only have perceptions changed and rights to a sexual life developed, but also contraceptive methods are more refined. Sterilisation for the purpose of purely preventing pregnancy (as opposed to medical reasons) generally requires a legal judgment to be made in the UK. Sterilisation in itself does not prevent or reduce individual desire for sexual activity or the libido.

Termination of pregnancy is not uncommon among non-spectrum women and requires two independent doctors to allow the procedure to take place as well as the consent of the woman, unless it can be shown medically that she cannot consent.

BREAST EXAMINATION AND MAMMOGRAMS

Breast examination is where autistic women's self-awareness comes into play. If parents enable their girls to know their own bodies, to see themselves in full-length mirrors, so they appreciate the totality of their body shapes, parents give them skills to spot when something is different and potentially 'wrong'. Most women have one breast slightly larger than the other, some have nipples that point outwards from the centre of their bodies and some have very dark areola (the skin of and around the nipple). These and other features become familiar to autistic women if they are encouraged to view themselves in private in their bedroom or locked bathroom alone.

If women see that one nipple is weeping fluid or is misshapen, this can indicate infection, pregnancy or other medical condition. Others may not see autistic women naked so it is critical for their health that they understand what is normal for them and what is different, and tell a trusted other or go to a doctor.

Teaching severely autistic females how to feel for lumps in their breasts after each period will enable them to detect early if they have any form of lump, due to infection, benign or malignant tumours. If they learn to do this as a routine, they will continue into adulthood when malignancies are more likely.

CERVICAL SMEARS AND EXAMINATIONS

If at all possible, parents need to introduce their daughters to cervical examinations as a concept, even if they do not immediately need one. The cervical screening programme in the UK invites all women from the age of 25 onwards for routine smear tests. There is specific information for parents of young women with intellectual disabilities at www.cancerscreening.nhs.uk/cervical/faq10.html.

If autistic women are to live long and healthy lives, the cervical screening programme is part of that, but cannot be achieved if they are unable or unwilling to have a cervical smear, which entails a vaginal speculum being inserted before an instrument which is used to scrape some cells from the cervix (at the top of the vagina). These cells are sent for laboratory tests.

Jane Keeling (2006), a practice nurse and mother of a severely autistic son, reported one case of a woman in her fifties with intellectual disabilities, who kept presenting at the doctors' surgery because she had urinary incontinence. Eventually, she was persuaded to have a smear; she had cervical cancer. Until that point, this woman had never had a cervical smear (Keeling 2006).

Even severely autistic women can be shown visually what will happen during a smear using available resources (see Resources). Parents can teach them how to concentrate on breathing while the examination takes place, which will enable them to more easily relax the vaginal muscles. Liaison with the practice nurse can result in agreement about signs or gestures that can be used by non-verbal women to signal 'wait' or 'stop'.

USING PUBLIC LAVATORIES

It is a useful exercise for parents to discuss what to do in a public lavatory before they attend one with their daughters. Understanding etiquette is important for autistic women to manage without their parents in future and is key to their independence. There are certain behaviours which they should be aware of as acceptable:

- Chatting is OK when outside the cubicle ('stall' to US readers). In fact it is commonplace to discuss make-up or clothing while washing hands and looking in the mirror.

- Chatting ceases once a woman is in the cubicle, unless one woman is asking another for toilet paper, which might be passed under the dividing wall, or unless two friends are in the lavatories and continuing conversation while they use the cubicles.

- Eye contact is usual and acceptable (although it might not be that usual for a woman with autism).

- Do not remove any clothing before entering the cubicle.

- Do not comment on one's own experience or activity in the cubicle – this is private information.

- Use the sanitary bin provided if necessary. Do not put sanitary pads or tampons down the lavatory.

- Wipe obvious blood or faeces off your fingers before leaving the cubicle.

- Replace all clothing fully before opening the door to the cubicle.

- Wash your hands thoroughly.

- Leave the lavatories.

CHAPTER 5

APPROPRIATE BEHAVIOUR

Although the goal of parents may be to educate and socialise their severely autistic children as far as possible into safe, competent and confident social beings, they may find that they are tackling sexuality issues only when they have become a problem. This chapter outlines examples of the most common issues around sexuality and severe autism and suggests possible strategies to deal with these. These are approaches a family can use in the first instance. If problems are established and/or intractable, professional help from medical or psychiatric practitioners may be necessary.

Remember that an established inappropriate behaviour may take months or even years to resolve or reduce. However, the consequences of not addressing sexuality can mean that autistic children may:

- become more isolated because they cannot behave appropriately in public, such as public disrobing and aggression (Stokes and Kaur 2005)

- engage in inappropriate relationships, such as sexual obsessions with other people (Stokes and Kaur 2005)

- engage in sexually inappropriate sexual behaviours directed towards others (Ray *et al.* 2004)

- put themselves at risk of sexually transmitted infections and unwanted pregnancies

- be at greater risk of sexual abuse

- become involved with the judicial system as sex offenders: in the UK a person can be put on the sex offenders' register from 14 years of age.

Note that the building blocks of sense of self and self-esteem underpin all these behaviours. This chapter is primarily dealing with pressing issues surrounding sexuality, acknowledging that ideally sex education adheres to the hierarchy of sexual learning needs (see Figure 2 on page 77).

It is also worthwhile noting that severely autistic children do not have access to social networks, where non-spectrum children usually express their sexuality, so they may use other arenas to be sexual (Koller 2000). During puberty about 30 per cent of autistic young people have an increase of what are described as 'behaviours of concern' (Eaves and Ho 1996) and this may coincide with a general increase in their social interest (McGovern and Sigman 2004).

The broader effects of these behaviours can include the following:

- Parents cannot socialise at home with friends or family with any sense of relaxation, or at all.

- Parents cannot invite guests to stay overnight.

- Our other children cannot enjoy having friends home to play, socialise or stay overnight.

- Parents can become trapped at home and socially isolated.

- Our other children may miss out on family activities and days out because parents cannot leave the home.

- Nursing or other caring agencies will not offer a respite service if children's behaviours are sexualised in a way that might place their staff in an unsafe situation.

MASTURBATION

For women, masturbation serves the same purposes as for men. They may use objects vaginally and touch their own breasts and nipples as part of masturbation.

However, touching breasts can be due to ill-fitting bras or ones with itchy material over the nipples, drawing the person's attention to their breasts.

Masturbation is a common sexual activity; the figures from research among people with intellectual disabilities suggest that the proportional difference between men and women reaching orgasm is similar to that of the mainstream population (Masters and Johnson 1988). The same research found that 74 per cent of men and 54 per cent of women masturbated, while other research has found no difference between genders in this respect (Haracopos and Pedersen 1992). The latter study found that there was a strong correlation between the frequency of masturbation and the person being able to achieve orgasm (Haracopos and Pedersen 1992).

So if autistic children are allowed time and privacy to masturbate, this will aid their ability to orgasm and prevent some of the difficulties associated with sexual frustration. There was also an apparent inverse relationship between lack of communication skills and frequency of masturbation. So the less able the person, the more masturbation they engaged in. Of course, it could be that more skilled communicators simply did not inform researchers of their private sexual activities or were more likely to be able to forge intimate relationships, which reduced their need for masturbation.

About 74 per cent of 14–17-year-old males masturbate; this increases with age and lower frequency of sexual intercourse with a partner (Gerressu *et al.* 2008). Although only 55 per cent of adolescent males with intellectual disabilities reported ever having masturbated, this may reflect reluctance to report a behaviour to which they may have been given negative responses. Certainly, masturbation is a common pastime for both non-spectrum and autistic males and for many of them may be their only form of sex life.

Why Do Severely Autistic People Masturbate in Public?

There are many reasons why autistic people masturbate in public, including the following:

- They don't understand the concept of private and public.

- They enjoy the sensory sensation.

- They have poor understanding of or empathy for others' feelings.

- They don't appreciate the idea of choices (to publicly masturbate) leading to consequences (being arrested by the police).

- They associate certain objects with masturbation, for example they may associate it with porcelain because they have been allowed to masturbate in the lavatory at home, so the sight of anything porcelain leads directly to a desire and expectation of masturbation.

- They associate certain activities with masturbation, for example whenever they undress, they masturbate, which may include when they visit public swimming pools.

This behaviour can occur in various settings, so it is important for parents to liaise with school, clubs and all caregivers to give the same message to their children, using the same words or symbols to reinforce it. Although we may understand the term 'masturbation', it is probably better to use explicit but correct language, such as 'Tom wants to touch his penis' in a social story or comic strip explaining where or how to do it.

Many parents wait until their severely autistic children start to masturbate before they consult with school or seek help to reduce or stop the behaviour. Parents may have strong moral or religious feelings about masturbation itself, which can provoke them to respond critically and overwhelmingly to the behaviour, inducing immense feelings of guilt if or when their children continue to masturbate, even into adulthood.

If masturbation has happened in a public place, parents' immediate reaction, in desperation to stop the actions, might be to chastise their children or pull their hands away. Although this probably will stop them continuing to masturbate at that moment, it also sends the message that sexuality and touching oneself is a bad thing. The goal of interventions should be to redirect children to the appropriate place (their bedrooms with the door shut and/or locked).

Timetabling opportunities to masturbate into children's days will have an immediate impact on the likelihood that they will try to do this in public places, because masturbation is incorporated into their routine. Research has found that the nature of autism, involving a critical need for predictability and lack of imagination, causes many to require fixed patterns of events in order to be sexually aroused (Ashkenazy and Yergeau 2013). So autistic sons may have sexual desire only when they see pictures of women in short skirts, or autistic daughters only when they watch a man smoking a cigarette. This aspect of sexuality can be harnessed to enable children to contain sexual behaviours to socially accepted places and times, preventing public displays.

If severely autistic people wear incontinence pads or inaccessible clothing, these should be removed for the timetabled period of masturbation, which needs to be generous. They may be able to dress themselves afterwards and clean up their own sexual body fluids, which will alert parents to the end of their need for private time. However, many of our autistic people cannot do either of these things, so parents may need to find a method of quietly checking if they have finished masturbating without interrupting the activity and preventing climax. In terms of cleaning up, parents need to try to remember that this is as much a part of their caring activities as cleaning their children after they have been incontinent – and there are major pluses for parents, in their being far less likely to touch their genitals in public if they can do so in private.

Research certainly has shown that many people with intellectual disabilities feel guilty about masturbating, partly because they do not understand that it is practised by the mainstream population. One of the greatest impacts on this negative feeling is if men or women who are valued in these autistic people's lives are able to state that they themselves masturbate. There are also resources which treat masturbation as it is, common and natural (see Resources).

It will help if parents observe in order to understand their children's triggers for masturbation, such as:

- the end of the day

- during periods of anxiety

- sensory overload in loud or crowded environments

- separation from a parent

- changes to routine, such as moving house or a new baby in the family

- obscure factors, for example painted toe nails, silver or glittery objects.

Intrinsic to autism is an essential need for predictability and a lack of social imagination. These two factors can combine to produce ritualised behaviours around sexual acts. Some severely autistic children may need an exact scenario in order to masturbate successfully, involving specific 'props'. For example, they may need to wear a certain coat or footwear and listen to or watch a clip from a particular piece of music or movie. Without these, they cannot achieve or maintain an erection or relax into clitoral stimulation and cannot reach climax.

If parents attempt to alter their sexual behaviours by removing these vital props, they run the risk of their children becoming frustrated and possibly aggressive or self-injurious. They are likely to replace their chosen objects with something similar, even if this means wandering out in the night when they suddenly discover them missing.

Masturbation can fulfil several functions for severely autistic people, which are largely self-soothing or 'stimming':

- to provide their only source of pleasure, excitement and gratification

- to relieve loneliness from social isolation

- to relieve anxiety and/or depression

- to relieve anger and/or frustration

- to provide physical pleasure

- to assist in relaxation

- to relieve sexual tension

- to help get to sleep

- to relieve genital discomfort

- to alleviate pain

- to relieve boredom

- to provide one of the few activities when they are not dependent on others.

Masturbation may also be a reaction to:

- having an infection

- needing their genital area washed

- wearing uncomfortable or tight underwear

- seeing an adult masturbating in the house or in movies or on the internet

- attempting to connect with peers

- suffering sexual abuse

- feeling the effects of medication, which can increase libido or reduce ability to climax causing frustration.

Regular masturbation, even daily, is common among non-spectrum adults and many of the above factors apply equally to this population. The difficulties for severely autistic people arise when they publicly masturbate, which can be for a wide variety of reasons, such as:

- lack of timetabled routine and time for masturbation

- lack of sexual opportunities

- lack of sex education, including understanding concepts of private and public

- lack of privacy in bedrooms, either due to sharing a room or not being allowed to shut or lock the door

- lack of respect for the person's privacy by parents, siblings or paid caregivers

- restricted access to their own genital areas due to incontinence pads or restrictive clothes.

Injury and constant masturbation can result from the person being unable to climax, leading to frustration and repeated attempts at masturbation.

Lockhart *et al.* (2009) found that around 50 per cent of adults with intellectual disabilities regularly masturbated. It was considered 'sexually inappropriate' only in the following circumstances (Hingsburger 1994):

- It occurs in the public arena.

- It causes self-injury.

- A person engages in it so much that the activity interferes with daily living.

Ways to Enable Severely Autistic People to Have Fulfilling and Safe Masturbatory Experiences

Here are some ways to enable autistic people to enjoy safe masturbation:

- Teach them about private versus public sexual behaviours.

- Timetable masturbation into their daily activities at home, for example ask them when they return from school, college or day centre if they want to 'touch penis', using the same symbol and words each time.

- Give them privacy in their bedrooms with the door shut and locked if possible, using a lock that could be unlocked from the outside in an emergency.

- Ensure that others in the home, including siblings, do not interrupt.

- Read leaflets or stories to them about how to masturbate to climax (see Resources). Use whatever resources they are used to, so this may be a series of picture jigs showing masturbating to climax and how to clean up afterwards. There are also anatomically correct dolls. Liaising with the school is helpful.

- Give them water-based lubricants to prevent abrasion and tissues or wipes to clean up after climax.

- Provide them with alternatives to comfort themselves when in a public place, such as cuddle toys or sensory materials which they can squeeze and manually manipulate.

- Ensure that their clothing is comfortable around the genital area to prevent them focusing attention on the area. Check if the clothing itself is causing them sexual stimulation – if it is not too loose, tight or folded.

- If they use objects anally to accelerate ejaculation, make these 'safe' by buying a recognised sexual toy, such as a vibrator (see Resources). Tactile sensors in and around the anus make the area highly sensitive.

UNSAFE OBJECTS USED IN SEXUAL ACTS

Non-spectrum adolescents and adults undoubtedly use objects during sexual acts, whether this is a vibrator (a battery-powered or rechargeable vibrating, usually penis-shaped device) or other sex toy, or whether it is a household or domestic object. From my experience as a sexual health counsellor, the latter may be anything from a glass bottle or deodorant canister to groceries, such as a banana, carrot or chocolate bar.

Any of these objects might be inserted into the vagina or anus for sexual arousal, either as a solo activity or in sex between partners. Sometimes objects are planned for use in a repertoire of sexual activity between partners, but at times they may simply be used opportunistically, being the only items to hand.

Now to consider severely autistic children: acknowledging that they have specific difficulties creating and maintaining friendships, let alone relationships, they may engage in solo sexual acts. This may be masturbation using a hand and digits or may involve an object to intensify the experience, or sometimes, if a male, to ejaculate quickly by rectally inserting an object while masturbating. This may be encouraged if men think they might be interrupted.

Depending on their functioning level, severely autistic people may be unable to access 'legitimate' sex toys, such as vibrators, which can be readily purchased on the high street or online. Buying these items is of course dependent on where our children live. If they live with parents, what would their attitudes be? If they live in a residential institution, it may be that such an object would be delivered by post and not be passed onto them, at least not without restrictions being imposed. These attitudinal and structural obstacles may mean that severely autistic people turn to domestic objects for sexual satisfaction and these may be unsuitable or even dangerous. For example, lids of canisters might be abrasive to the vaginal or anal walls, while food items might cause candida albicans (thrush) or fungal infection. Hard objects such as pots might be utilised, possibly causing bruising or other injury.

Autism involves many sensory issues and this can be important in sexuality in which stimulation of the senses can act as sexual arousal. Tactile senses may increase the likelihood of certain materials being used, such as leather belts, silky underwear or rubber gloves. Olfactory sense (smell) may ensure that a particular fragrance, dirty underwear or the smell of cigarettes always pre-empts sexual acts. Visual senses may dictate that bare arms or certain coloured or styled hair stimulate sexual arousal. Knowing that autistic people have rigid thinking and adhere to routines, once established using specific rituals, it can be difficult to move them onto other, more suitable sex enhancers.

How to Address the Use of Unsafe Objects

If there isn't an established pattern of sexual arousal, pre-empt possible use of unsuitable objects by purchasing 'official' sex toys. These are available to order via the Family Planning Association (see Resources). Parents can involve their children in the process of choosing items, which they will be using. This consultation enhances their sense of self-esteem because they are involved in the decision-making and lessens any sense of guilt they might harbour for masturbating or engaging in sexual acts.

Parents can introduce water-based lubricants, which are easily available in pharmacies. Safer toys can be introduced by engaging autistic people in choosing sex toys.

Enable autistic children to 'contain' their special sexual interests. For example, if they attach a certain fragrance or smell with sexual arousal, provide it for use in their bedrooms. Containing or restraining sexual urges in public is, after all, what many non-spectrum people do. With autistic children, parents may need to give them strategies to do the same.

TOUCHING OTHER PEOPLE INAPPROPRIATELY

Inappropriate behaviour includes touching other people's private body parts, such as breasts, buttocks or genital areas. Often this involves frottage, or rubbing sexual areas of the body against others through clothing. Sometimes the autistic person might touch another person whom they may or may not know while touching their own genital area. It can include stroking another's hair, which may seem an innocuous thing to do but can be regarded as sexual assault if it is done to a stranger.

It is worth assessing what behaviours parents allow at home and envisaging these in public areas or with people you do not know. Autistic people have difficulty differentiating between what is acceptable in different arenas, so they will expect to be able to do the same things wherever they are, unless parents can instil in them understanding. When parents have children who do not readily touch or hug them, they may gain a level of closeness they have not had before if the child strokes the parent's hair.

How to Address Inappropriate Touching of Other People

Parents should work through what areas of the body are private. Parents may need to explain the meaning of the 'private' parts of the body that no one else sees unless they are ill and a doctor needs to examine them, or they are being cared for by a caregiver (who may be the parents) or someone they are in an intimate relationship with.

Parents can use a 'body zone' chart which identifies visually which parts of the body on women and men are private. Some autistic children respond with greater understanding if colours are used and it will be helpful to liaise with schools to see how they mark a 'no go' area. They may use red signs, for example, so parents can use 'red zones' pictorially to show private body zones. For other autistic children, colours are distracting, so black and white pictures are better.

Figure 1 (page 59) showing the circles of connections and contacts can be used to explain connections to the autistic person in society and how some people (close family) can be touched and others, on the outer circles (depicting friends, acquaintances or strangers) should never be touched in their private body zones and greeted with a handshake or high five.

Parents should work through the 'arm's length' rule (see Chapter 2). Parents can use picture jigs or story (Manasco and Manasco 2012) to explain that some people do not like being touched at all.

PUBLIC DISROBING

Public disrobing includes stripping off some or all clothing in public places, such as shopping centres, or in shared parts of the home, such as the sitting room. This may never have happened before puberty or may be an established behaviour in the home, held over from childhood when parents were trying to toilet train a severely autistic child.

How to Address Public Disrobing

Make a note of when this happens, examine and act on possible triggers. Try not to be emotive. Think about the following:

- What are the house rules about wearing or not wearing clothes? Do the rules need to be altered?

- Is the child's underwear comfortable in terms of size, fabric and style? Too small underpants will make a son's testicles hot or may dig in; both will cause a child to want to remove them. Ill-fitting bras cause similar discomfort. If the fabric is itchy, or the underwear is either brand new or very tatty and old, this could be uncomfortable. In terms of style, boxer shorts can sometimes wrinkle up or pull on testicles or pubic hair, for example.

- Has this only started since puberty? Autistic children may be distressed by the growth of pubic hair, which may be felt more when covered with clothing or by the growth in children's genitalia. Changing the style of underwear may alleviate the problem.

- If the disrobing involves the upper body, this may be due to the sensation of clothing against underarm hair or tender nipples and breasts. Looser clothing, trimming or shaving the hair might help; just explaining what is happening might improve the situation. If young women's breasts are tender, check that the bra is well fitted with soft fabric inside, rather than lace, which can catch on nipples. Make sure young women are warm enough since erect nipples are more likely to rub fabric. If nothing else works, it may be necessary to use mild forms of analgesia (pain killers) in the short term while young women are developing during puberty.

- Has disrobing only started since a daughter started menstruating? She may be uncomfortable with damp sanitary pads or other sensations caused by the process of menstruating. She may have abdominal cramps or be extremely hot due to hormone levels during her period.

- Is disrobing linked with wearing incontinence pads? Autistic children may be distressed by being damp with urine or faeces for even a short amount of time.

NON-CONSENSUAL HUGGING

Non-consensual hugging tends to be more of a problem for young people with other intellectual difficulties, because inherent to autism are sensory issues, such as touch, which can inhibit any willingness to be close to others. However, autism parents may find quite the opposite in their children, who may rush up to others, either bowling them over for a hug or just bear-hugging.

This behaviour may seem like over-exuberance and cuddles when closeness may have been something parents have longed for in their relationship with their autistic child. But small children, elderly relatives and others may be hurt due to these behaviours, especially as the 'child' may be a fully grown, strong adult. At the very least parents may find people avoiding them and their autistic child; at worst, the police may become involved due to claims of physical assault.

The recipient may not seem reluctant; after all many friends and family want to support parents and not create more problems for them than they already have. But allowing this behaviour not only opens the door for sexual and other abuse from others, but also may facilitate children becoming inappropriately sexual with others because they know no boundaries to intimate behaviours.

How to Address Non-consensual Hugging

- Look for triggers and try to work out what purpose the behaviour serves for the child.

- Enlist the support of friends, relatives and others who work with the child, so they do not unwittingly increase this unwanted behaviour by laughing it off or smiling after it has happened.

- Work through the circles of connections and contacts, looking specifically at greetings. Bear-hugging and bowling others off their feet should not feature as a greeting for anyone.

- Teach the 'arm's length' rule and practise it as a game. Enlist friends and family to be greeted in the different appropriate ways for where they are in children's lives, according to the circles of connections and contacts.

- Keep any response to inappropriate greetings as low key as possible, without shouting or dramatic actions. Focus on the 'victims' of the unwanted behaviours. Often autistic children will receive social attention, even if it is negative, for unsocial behaviours, which reinforces the very behaviours parents are trying to stop.

- Reward behaviours where the child does not bear-hug and bowl someone over, using something you know the child values, that is, use positive reinforcement of desired behaviours.

INAPPROPRIATE BEHAVIOURS

Sometimes the motivation behind autistic children's behaviours might be misinterpreted. In each of the following examples, the information should be given in the most accessible way for the child, involving repetition and assessing how much the child has understood. The examples tend to occur when the foundations of sex education have not been laid, and issues arise as the child grows older.

Predatory Behaviour

A severely autistic son who follows young boys around might be seen as a sexual predator. It could alarm and frighten any children involved, but more likely their parents. Yet this behaviour could be the autistic man's only way of socialising in a world where he has no peers who are willing to socialise with him. Young boys may talk with him, and in a less challenging way than peers would.

HOW TO ADDRESS PREDATORY BEHAVIOUR

- Work through the circles of connections or contacts to show the son that he shouldn't be talking to strangers (even if they are younger) and that they shouldn't be talking with him. Ensure that he is aware that these children's parents could involve the police if they are concerned about his talking with little children, even if his parents realise he doesn't mean them harm.

- Help the son find social clubs or outlets with adults with whom he can talk. Sometimes parents assume their severely autistic children are too locked in their own world to need or want social contacts, especially as forging these links can be onerous and difficult when there are barriers such as lack of facilities and transport.

- Help to keep him occupied. Often boredom or loneliness can lead to autistic children seeking entertainment and company.

Stalking Behaviour

A severely autistic daughter watches one non-spectrum male whenever he is in a public area, follows him in the street and waits outside his home for him to appear. From this description one could see a police case for stalking. The woman's perspective may be that she loves this man, even if they have never spoken and he has a wife and family. Her desire for a relationship, which has not been fulfilled in reality, becomes achievable in this fantasy. The obsessive nature of these behaviours fits neatly with an autistic person's critical need for predictability. Lack of social imagination and insight into others' emotions or how her behaviours might impact on others ensure that her actions would persist without external intervention.

HOW TO ADDRESS STALKING BEHAVIOUR

- Help the daughter access social activities where she can associate with peers. Increase her social circle and keep her busy with social attention.

- Work through the circle of connections and contacts and examine where she thinks this man is compared to her on the circle, then address the reality of this, placing him where he should be on the circle (a stranger).

- Work through the idea of feelings, starting with hers, which she may be able to access if she's in love. Then discuss the man's feelings and how he might feel that a stranger is following him. Work out how she will manage being rejected; this may be with anger and/or self-injurious behaviours initially. It is probably better not to involve the fact that he has a family as a reason for his being unavailable, in case her obsession with him becomes an obsession to remove them.

- Be clear that her behaviours will be seen as criminal under stalking laws, if she continues and that the police might become involved.

- E Friending is a service provided by the National Autistic Society in the UK, which is helpful if autistic children have computing skills.

Exposure of Genitalia

A son at the severe end of the autism spectrum exposes his penis to his parents and encourages them to look at it or guides their hands towards his genitals with or without clothing in an apparent desire to be touched. Despite first appearance, this may not be sexual in origin. Parents should consider whether their son has behaved similarly with other non-sexual parts of his body to alert them to health issues, such as rashes or pain. The son may be experiencing spontaneous erections or changes to his genital area which he finds alarming, such as growth of pubic hair and the enlargement of his penis and testicles. Drawing his parents' attention to the genital area could be to 'tell' them of his distress.

If this is sexual in nature, it should be seen in the context of the young man's level of development in terms of communication and cognitive abilities. Remember that very young non-spectrum children will explore their sexuality by touching their own genitals, sometimes allowing their peers of either gender to look at or touch them also. In such children, parents may accept this as part of their development, even if they do not encourage them to do so. With our adolescent or adult autistic children, they may be experimenting in a similar way, which fits their functioning level of communication and cognitive abilities and uses the people they find themselves surrounded by – the family, visiting friends, sometimes people in public places.

HOW TO ADDRESS EXPOSURE OF GENITALIA

- Check for a medical problem and seek medical advice.

- Use picture jigs and stories to explain unwanted erections, wet dreams and physical changes that take place.

- Work through what are private and public places and parts of the body, as above.

- Build into the boy's schedule time for masturbation and self-exploratory behaviours in the privacy of his bedroom with the door shut and/or locked.

- Work through the circles of connections or contacts, as above.

Public Disrobing

A severely autistic adolescent son strips off all his lower clothing whenever he is home, puts his feet through the arms of his shirt instead of wearing trousers and refuses to dress otherwise. This may be interpreted as public disrobing (public because it is in shared parts of the home). In the context of home, this is totally disruptive because no guests can be invited there and the behaviour can be distressing to the rest of the family. The man's perspective might be that the growth of pubic hair on his penis and testicles feels uncomfortable against any item of clothing. Wearing the shirt with his feet through the arms feels like he has trousers on without the continuously distressing feeling of clothing against his genitals.

HOW TO ADDRESS PUBLIC DISROBING

- Work through private versus public behaviours and body parts.

- Try out other underwear, such as boxer shorts, to see if this helps.

- Try out loose trousers, such as track suit bottoms, without underwear. Try out very soft cotton trousers which aren't hot and don't have the sensory issues associated with harder fabrics.

- Encourage the son to spend time in his bedroom without his bottom half of clothing on, with the door shut and/or locked. This may enable him to tolerate clothing more when in public places.

- Consider enabling him to trim his pubic hair to see if a shorter length might reduce the sensory distress being caused. The whole issue may be temporary and may abate once all pubic hair has grown and is less itchy.

- Comic strip stories can be helpful to explain feelings around behaviours (see Resources).

Spontaneous Masturbation

A severely autistic daughter immediately touches her own genitals and breasts whenever she sees a man with a naked chest. She may or may not strip off her clothing. This can be anywhere, including public places such as the seaside, swimming pool or in the street. For the general public, this is exposure or indecent behaviour. For the young woman, it is a sexual impulse to which she's responding.

HOW TO ADDRESS SPONTANEOUS MASTURBATION

- Work through what are public and private behaviours and parts of the body.

- Locate precisely what the trigger is for this behaviour. It may seem obvious that it is a man's chest; however, it may be the nature of that particular chest that is key. For example, is it a hairy chest or not? What colour are the chest hairs? What colour is the skin? Use pictures from magazines or newspapers or similar to enable your daughter to exactly describe the trigger.

- Create a book of cuttings of precisely the trigger chests (or whatever it is, in your child's case). The daughter can have timetabled into her day a period when she can look at her 'Chest Book' and masturbate in her bedroom with the door shut and/or locked.

- Make a picture jig of the Chest Book, so if the daughter starts to touch her genitals in response to a man's chest in public, parents can show her the picture and say that she can go home now to look at the book and 'touch vagina and breasts'.

These triggers can seem obscure, such as silver pots, nail varnish or toe rings, and are often related to the fact that autistic children have sensory issues. The key is to be open-minded and precise in discovering triggers.

Unwanted Sexual Advances

A pre-pubescent son suddenly starts rubbing his hands on his mother's breasts through clothing when she is in her bedroom. For her, this is distressing and an assault. For him, he is responding to an impulse.

HOW TO ADDRESS UNWANTED SEXUAL ADVANCES

- Thinking as the mother, what was the exact scenario when this occurred? What was she wearing? Where was she? What precisely did the son do? Sometimes the taboo of having a child, especially one of the opposite gender, feeling their bodies can blind parents to the possible causes of behaviours. Look for the purpose of the behaviour for the son. If the mother's clothing was unusual or different, perhaps for an evening out, the son might be fascinated by the fabric. Anything sheer or with silver or gold thread running through it might be a special interest for an autistic child. Did the son feel the mother's breasts or simply run his hands all over the material, maybe even rubbing his face close into it. These features would mark it as a sensory issue.

- Then answer the trigger found. If it is a particular fabric, enable the son to show which materials fascinate him and buy some small samples. If his impulse is not sexual in nature (he doesn't touch his genitals when holding or rubbing the fabric, for example), parents can let him simply have the samples as a comforter wherever he is. This is relatively common in non-spectrum children, not just in autism.

- If the son simply ran into the bedroom, parents can introduce or reintroduce the notion of private rooms into their house rules. These can be reinforced by teaching him scripts, such as 'May I come in?' to which parents must reply 'Yes, you may' before he is allowed in a private area like a bedroom. All the family should be involved in reinforcing these house rules.

- If the behaviour is sexual, work through private body zones (as above).

- Allow private time for the child to be alone and sexual in his bedroom.

SMEARING

Smearing behaviour includes severely autistic people putting their hands into faeces in their nappies (diapers), smearing faeces over everything, such as their own bodies, every piece of furniture or other people, and defecating anywhere they find themselves. This behaviour is immensely distressing to parents and caregivers and can cause untold emotional harm to siblings, who cannot bring friends home, who dare not go out publicly with their severely autistic brothers and live in a highly charged and stressful household due to their parents' anger and distress.

There are several possible explanations for smearing behaviour, none of which is to be vindictive to parents, despite it feeling like that is the reason. Autistic children may enjoy the smell and texture of faeces, which feeds their need for sensory input. This may result in them rubbing faeces on their faces for an intense smell sensation, squeezing it between their fingers. It may be sexual, if our children are trying to reach their genitals or anus, which are highly sensitive areas. Smearing is perceived by parents as a shameful activity which is not openly discussed, despite it being the experience of many with severely autistic children.

Closely linked to smearing is picking at nappies or diapers, often resulting in scattered pieces of disposable nappies or absorbent gel. This can be wearisome and debilitating for parents. Again, the first way to tackle this is to observe for triggers. These are usually sensory or sexual in basis, or due to lack of other interesting things to do.

Ways to Tackle Smearing and Picking Based on Observation for Possible Triggers

- If the cause is discomfort, this is a hard lesson in more regular changing of nappies or diapers. If children are so aware of feeling uncomfortable in soiled clothing, it may be worth parents revisiting toilet training, since the recognition of being soiled is a good prerequisite for continence.

- If the cause is sensory, parents can give an alternative to faeces, such as play dough, which can be enhanced with fragrance and, if home-made, can be edible. For various recipes for play dough, go to http://babyparenting.about.com/cs/activities/a/ playdough.htm.

- In picking behaviours, try alternative sensory choices, such as squeeze balls.

- If the cause is boredom, clean up without speaking or 'rewarding' with an activity such as the television. Instead, when the children are clean between episodes, keep them busy with activities they enjoy or are totally absorbing.

- If there appears to be a sexual basis, parents can schedule into their children's days a period when they can be nappy or diaper free and undisturbed in their own bedrooms. This will give them time to explore their genital areas and masturbate or sexually satisfy themselves. Timetabled sexual time should lessen children's need to explore sexually at other times. Parents may not enjoy having to clean up semen or female body fluids after children have masturbated. However, this may be better than the impromptu clearing up of faeces and nappy contents, especially in public places.

- Some practitioners and other parents will advocate dressing children in all-in-one jump suits, back-to-front clothes (so the fastenings are at the back) or belts or trousers with buttoned flies if children have poor fine motor skills. I have even seen duct tape recommended for strapping 'Houdini' children into nappies. However, I would expect that following the suggestions above will diminish if not completely remove the problem.

- There are comprehensive resources to help parents, including a story to read to the children (see Resources).

CHALLENGING BEHAVIOURS

Behaviours are classified as challenging when they affect the person's quality of life or they compromise the individual's or others' safety. The likelihood of challenging behaviours occurring is increased if someone has autism, sensory deficits and poor communication skills.

Challenging behaviours might include:

- aggression, such as head butting, hitting, kicking, scratching or biting

- destruction, such as throwing objects, smashing items or tearing clothing

- self-injurious actions, such as head banging, skin or nail picking or biting the self

- pica, which is eating inedible objects, such as cigarette butts and faeces.

In relation to sexuality, these behaviours can occur for the following reasons:

- rejection of sexual advances or interest, resulting in self-injurious, destructive or aggressive acts

- in conjunction with sexual acts as part of a ritual, such as an individual hitting his penis hard with a leather belt to induce erection.

Only the most extreme of challenging behaviours, which might result in serious injury, require medication. The majority of behaviours can be managed by keeping a diary to locate triggers that usually fall into the following categories:

- medical reasons

- need for attention

- need for particular items

- trying to avoid a situation

- sensory issues.

Medical Reasons

In sexuality this could be aggression as a result of infection or inflammation causing self-injurious behaviours. Epilepsy or common infections such as urinary tract infections can result in aggression or self-injury.

Need for Attention

Whether positive or negative responses, severely autistic children may use challenging behaviours to achieve their own desires or goals for attention.

Need for Particular Items

Poor communication skills can mean that severely autistic children learn to gain what they need by particular behaviours, which parents may inadvertently reinforce by their responses. For example, if their children do not have privacy or time to explore themselves sexually, they may act aggressively due to frustration, which may cause us to place them in their bedroom alone. Parents may see this as a quiet area for them to reduce anxieties and self-calm. For the child this may be their opportunity to masturbate without disturbance. The end result may promote the challenging behaviour because the child has gained what he/she needs.

Trying to Avoid a Situation

Challenging behaviours such as pica, especially if this involves eating faeces, can cause parents to isolate the autistic child. Again, this may be the desired outcome for the child, so the child repeats the challenging behaviour.

Sensory Issues

Severely autistic children use stimming or self-stimulatory actions to alleviate anxiety in stressful situations. For example, rocking, head banging, rubbing the groin and jumping repetitively afford them sensory input. Sometimes a sound might give a similar sensory experience, for example clicking the tongue or finger joints.

Strategies for Intervention in Challenging Behaviours

If safe to do so, parents should ignore the behaviour or respond in a very low arousal manner which offers no 'rewards' for the behaviours. Parents can change the situation using distraction or diversion. Whatever they do, they should do so quickly so that they do not reinforce persistence in the behaviours.

Early intervention in challenging behaviours can prevent them from becoming entrenched and more severe in nature, in terms of personal injury or harm to others. Key goals of intervention should include the following:

- Improving communication skills, using whatever methods produce results. This may be the Picture Exchange Communications System (PECS) (Baker 2000), Makaton signing, social stories and comic strips (Gray 2000), picture jigs or using intensive interaction to promote self-esteem and relationships as a foundation of all other learning including communication skills (see Chapter 2). Research has shown a clear inverse relationship between lack of communication skills and self-injurious behaviours, that is, the less able the children are at expressing their needs, the more likely they are to self-harm (Dominick *et al.* 2007).

- Using low arousal responses to challenging behaviours, thus no shouting or physical response to the child.

- Trying to understand the motivation for behaviours and removing, as far as is possible, the emotion we attach to them. This can be extremely difficult, particularly if behaviours are public or seem personal and sexual.

- Agreeing within the family on how to respond in a consistent manner to challenging behaviours. Use routine language and standard picture jigs each time.

GENERAL PRINCIPLES FOR WHAT PARENTS SHOULD DO

Parents should try to do the following:

- Remove their emotions from the event or incident.

- Keep a careful diary of any incidents or sexualised behaviours.

- Identify triggers or note the exact scenario in which the behaviour took place, including location, what else was happening or had just happened and what time of day.

- Be aware that what appear to be sexualised behaviours may not have sex as the purpose.

- Be specific about what behaviours their children are displaying. Are they touching someone else on every part of the body or just the erogenous zones, for example?

Once parents have located the triggers and motivation for behaviours, they should try to replicate these in the safety and privacy of the children's bedroom. For example, create a box of 'trigger' fabrics, textures or colours so that their children can have allocated time to enjoy sensory experiences while masturbating. Parents can get their children to help make a book of the very specific triggers that cause arousal, such as pink painted finger nails, and give the children time in their bedroom to enjoy the book, removing it when their children have climaxed.

Another possibility, once triggers are located, is to replicate aspects of the behaviours which children enjoy, but in a safe way. For example, if their children eat faeces for sensory reasons, try a similar textured play dough with a heavy smell and taste. Or try an alternative oral stimulant, like chewing gum or specialised chewing materials (see Resources). This is referred to as 'differential reinforcement'. It can also be applied to incompatible actions which prevent the unwanted behaviours. For example, if their children squeeze their crotches in public, assuming there is no medical cause, having them hold squeeze balls in each hand and rewarding this behaviour should stop the focus on the crotch.

Parents should have specific picture jigs with them when in public places, which refer directly to any sexualised behaviours, such as a picture card stating 'Do you want to touch vagina/penis?' Then have one which tells the child to 'wait' and another to show that they are returning home to the child's bedroom. Once children are in a routine of regular masturbation or other sexual activity, they should have less need to suddenly and publicly need to satisfy arousal.

Parents should use standard verbal language and picture jigs each time and communication techniques with which their children are familiar. They should ensure that all family members and caregivers use the same strategies, responses and visual cueing.

CHAPTER 6

RECOGNISING AND REPORTING WHEN THINGS DON'T SEEM RIGHT

This chapter considers some of the difficult and worst possible scenarios for severely autistic children. It outlines measures that parents can take to minimise the likelihood of these happening in the first instance and how to manage them if they occur. The last section focuses on sexual abuse, which is one of the most feared of possibilities for parents.

NETWORK OF TRUSTED ADULTS

To maximise children's ability to report difficult or potentially dangerous situations, they need an established network of trusted and responsible adults. The wider this circle of contacts is, the better. It diminishes the chances of any individual breaching trust or behaving inappropriately towards these children.

Severely autistic children can be educated visually to understand who is in this circle of trusted contacts. They can also be informed who in authority can be approached or trusted. This would include the police, teachers and doctors, all of whom may become involved if sexual abuse is suspected. So-called 'autism passports', which identify for these professions when a person has autism, are becoming more commonly used. In addition, autism agencies in the UK are improving autism training given to staff in key areas, such as the police, so this should create a better response if sexual abuse or similar issues are reported either via third parties or by the autistic person. Support mechanisms should include the autistic person having a social worker or trained person attend with them at the police station before any questioning takes place. Policies and procedures around sexual abuse, sexual assaults and rape cases, including those involving 'vulnerable' people, such as severely autistic individuals, are well established in the UK.

In terms of what children can report to adults in their circles of connections and contacts, it could be anything from being sexually attracted to someone and asking how to pursue or manage these feelings to divulging that another person asked them to perform a sexual act. Trusted adults need to be aware of the possibilities and know what to do. Parents need to feel that any trusted adults will take their children seriously and not belittle any of their concerns.

Once parents have established a baseline of trusted contacts, these may need to be added to, as their children become adults. This is because some contacts may become unwell or die and parents need to ensure their children continue to have about the same size circle of trusted adults surrounding them. Parents must constantly look to the future.

HOW TO MANAGE REJECTION

Severely autistic children may feel friendless and isolated because of their difference from the non-spectrum population. Parents have a duty to try to expand their social contacts with peers and allow them to learn about friendships, even if this is painful at times. Rejection can be one of those times.

If they feel isolated, autistic children can be easily manipulated, which puts them at risk of sexual, emotional or financial abuse. Isolation also means they may yearn for emotional attachment to others with whom they may not even be acquainted. When their approach for friendship is not reciprocated, these children may feel intense rejection, sometimes resulting in aggression or self-injurious behaviours.

Locating and understanding feelings should be one of parents' basic lessons with their children, started at an early point in life (see Chapter 2). Another useful piece of work they can do with their children is to explain how they are different from other people. Many parents shy away from this because it is difficult to admit the difference. Some parents intellectualise the issue and assert that the social world should accommodate difference, and there is no need to emphasise that their children do not behave or communicate like the mainstream population.

What I would argue is that our children are better able to manage situations if they know they are different and why. If we read expositions by people with higher functioning autism or Asperger syndrome, they outline the importance of understanding how they function and how non-spectrum people do. This enables them to better manage their responses because they are less likely to misinterpret a non-spectrum person's behaviours. Severely autistic children may not be able to engage in social relationships to this level but they can be helped to recognise early signs of disinterest in others, so that they do not become too embroiled in a relationship that is only wanted on their side.

In the non-spectrum world, one of the ways we deal with rejection in relationships is to realise that we have other options and that we can develop other, more constructive relationships. If parents isolate their severely autistic children, they reduce any chance that they have of moving onto other friendships and their children will recognise this, become entrenched in destructive friendships or be less able to react positively to rejection of any sort.

Like any person, severely autistic children need space to express themselves when they feel rejected. This may not be how parents would; it may involve destructive, aggressive or self-injurious behaviours initially. It may not incorporate some level of communicating what happened because this is not usually easy or the first impulse.

HOW TO SAY 'NO' AND REJECT ANOTHER'S ADVANCES OR END RELATIONSHIPS

The ability to reject others, whether this is unwanted interest or to end relationships, depends largely on the children's awareness of what is 'right' behaviour and their sense of self-esteem. Practising saying 'no' and being heard and acted upon is a process parents can implement early in their children's lives over small issues, developing this into broader and more important issues.

The following are areas in which autistic children need to be clear what is appropriate behaviour:

- Touch: which parts of the body are private and who in one's circle of contacts may touch those parts, but only if the child says 'yes'.

- Body space: who in one's circle of connections should be at what distance (arm's length, hugging).

- Secrets: what they are and when they are not appropriate.

- Power within relationships and friendships.

PREGNANCY

Severely autistic children of either gender and their parents need to be aware of the signs of pregnancy:

- lack of menstruation, or very light periods

- tender breasts, nipple and breast enlargement (this also happens as young women develop during adolescence)

- nausea and vomiting

- fatigue and exhaustion.

Severely autistic adults should have an idea of which services are available and for what. Pregnancy can be reported via the family doctor or through family planning clinics and they can receive counselling about how to proceed. However, before this parents can educate their children so that they understand how to test for pregnancy early.

For parents of children whose cognitive abilities are too restricted to engage in this level of learning, if parents see any of the above signs of pregnancy, this could be the first sign that sexual abuse has happened. However, many of these symptoms can occur for other gynaecological reasons. Parents should seek medical advice.

SEXUALLY TRANSMITTED INFECTIONS

Severely autistic children should be aware of where to seek help if they think they might have sexually transmitted infections, either via the family doctor or the expertise in genitourinary medicine clinics. Parents should be aware of symptoms (see Chapter 2) and seek a medical opinion if their children are cognitively too challenged to do so.

RAPE

Parents need to make sure that as their autistic children grow into adults, they understand what rape is and what to do if this happens. Parents should remember to identify that rape can happen male to female, male to male and, on rare occasions, a female perpetrator can rape a male. As many autistic children are hands-on learners, it may be best to role-play or use life-like dolls to demonstrate some potentially dangerous situations. If children communicate non-verbally, parents can teach them clear signs to show a person to stop what they are doing.

Autistic people often cannot understand that others have their own thoughts and emotions; they believe that everyone thinks and feels what they do. Because of this, many are shocked to find that 'bad' people in the world will take advantage of sexual situations. Parents may need to explain to their autistic children what kinds of dress and conduct are appropriate in public so that they are not unwittingly attracting sexual attention.

If a rape has happened, or a parent suspects this, the victim (the autistic child) should not wash but should present at the family doctor, casualty at hospital, a rape crisis centre or at the police. Body fluids and physical examination would be critical for a criminal case. There would also be medical follow-up, including tests for possible sexually transmitted infections and pregnancy.

ABUSE BY CAREGIVERS

In terms of residential care, in the 2010 UK case of Winterbourne View care home, a television documentary sent in an undercover reporter who covertly filmed routine physical abuse of disabled residents by several members of staff. This well-publicised criminal behaviour has doubtless undermined parental trust in caregiving institutions, which, despite being smaller than their Victorian counterparts, still cultivate a culture in which abuse can flourish. Where parents might have considered trying to establish their profoundly autistic child in a residence away from the family home, overseen by caregivers, the Winterbourne View case may well have entrenched fears of abuse and consequently increased dependence of disabled children and young people on their parents.

Even in the community caregivers or members of the family can abuse severely autistic children. Sexual abuse certainly is more likely to be perpetrated by someone well known to the child, but children are also open to emotional abuse (e.g. manipulation by fear) and physical abuse (e.g. beatings).

In these scenarios the most important strategy is to ensure that a broad number of people are visiting and spending time with severely autistic children throughout their lifetime. This enhances the likelihood of abuse being spotted and as early as possible, especially if visits are impromptu. It also increases the opportunities for children to report or discuss what is happening in their lives. Some cases of abuse have been uncovered by relatives placing video cameras in rooms or on their children, which have recorded absolute evidence. Severely autistic children and adults may be unable to articulate what is happening and parents need to be their eyes and their voices. My personal experience of working in a range of nursing homes and hospitals is that the more articulate and vocal the patient or the more vigilant the relatives, the better care is provided and the more respect the patient is shown.

SEXUAL ABUSE

Across all children under the age of 18 years, around one in three girls and one in ten boys will be sexually abused (Tang, Freyd and Wang 2007). For those with developmental disabilities (not specifically autism) the numbers are believed to be twice as high and exacerbated by social isolation and alienation (Mansell, Sobsey and Moskal 1998). The case of now deceased Jimmy Savile, a television presenter in the UK, demonstrated that even non-spectrum children may not be believed when they attempt to report sexual assaults and abuse, including as adults. There is also the danger that Savile's behaviour will be dismissed because it was part of a different philosophy around sexual practices in the 1950s to 1990s. Parents need to continue to be vigilant and sensitive to sexual abuse.

Signs of Sexual Abuse

Note that it is difficult to assess if a severely autistic child has been sexually abused on observed behaviours alone. Some behaviours appear to be pathologised because they are not typical of non-spectrum behaviours; this is a good example of when verbal, more communicative autistic people can offer insight. Research has shown that some abused autistic children do not show any behaviours which would raise concerns (Kendall-Tackett, Williams and Finkelhor 1993).

Sexualised behaviours can indicate sexual abuse, but may be interpreted as delayed progression of non-spectrum sexual development. The children's attempts to understand or deal with sexual abuse may lead to exaggerated, more intense behaviours which they already practise, such as self-stimulatory behaviours (e.g. head banging, rocking, jumping), self-injury (e.g. biting, picking at fingers and skin) and repetitive actions, all of which are self-soothing activities.

Children may develop new behaviours. Non-verbal autistic children may display more behavioural difficulties and this may be directly related to frustration in trying to communicate and disclose abuse. Sexualised behaviours also can be a sign of physical abuse (Merrick *et al.* 2008).

The American Psychological Association (2013) identifies the following behaviours which are common in non-spectrum children who have been sexually abused:

- difficulties in sleeping and experiencing nightmares

- anxiety, depression, being withdrawn

- sexually transmitted infections, especially if the child is under 14 years old

- difficulty in walking or sitting

- angry outbursts, propensity to run away, refusal to change for gym or participate in sporting activities, sexual behaviours that are unusual or inappropriate for their age, regressive behaviours and reluctance to be left alone with certain individuals.

All of these features can occur in autism spectrum disorders in the absence of sexual abuse.

Signs that May Be Misinterpreted

If parents believe their children to be asexual, any sexualised behaviours may be misinterpreted as signs of sexual abuse. Certainly, research has found that those with learning difficulties were systematically excluded from full participation in the social world and believed to be asexual, so were not given opportunities for sex education and expression of sexuality, so any sexual displays were believed to indicate sexual abuse (Nario-Redmond 2010).

In addition, it is argued that sexual behaviours form a continuum and that they can be the result of generally traumatic events or over-stimulating environmental experiences, not just abuse of some sort (Cavanagh Johnson 2002).

Assessing Sexual Abuse

In cases of non-spectrum children, where sexual abuse is suspected, assessment depends on medical examination and forensic interview. Medical evidence is rare in cases of sexual abuse because it usually occurs chronically (over time) and is unlikely to be reported immediately after an episode has happened unless it is rape, physical violence is involved or the act has been witnessed.

At interview, a history of events by the child and family will be taken. Information from children relies on them being able to engage in an interview using verbal exchanges, following what the interviewer is asking or being able to accurately describe events, often over a lengthy one-off interview (Cronch, Viljoen and Hansen 2006).

Reporting requires 'referential communication' (Dahlgren and Dahlgren Sandberg 2008), which involves the person reporting sufficient information so that the listener knows to what he/she is referring. This research found that autistic children in general were less effective referential communicators, so had greater difficulty conveying what had happened in a way that would be understood by other people (Dahlgren and Dahlgren Sandberg 2008). One study found that some autistic children were challenged by pragmatic language and had difficulty maintaining conversation (Hale and Tager-Flusberg 2005). This is when it is imperative that parents have enabled their children as far as possible with sexual information so they have knowledge which can be accessed by communication specialists if sexual abuse occurs.

New approaches for autistic children are needed to assess if sexual abuse has happened (see Appendix 4).

Treatments

Perhaps in the past there was an assumption that our severely autistic children could not benefit from conventional therapies available to non-spectrum survivors of sexual abuse. Certainly, counsellors and therapists need to have experience and understanding of what the Autism Research Center (quoted in Autism Speaks 2013) describes as 'non-verbal mind-body healing modalities that do not require an intellectual processing component of the therapy', that is, communicated using visual aids, such as pictures, social stories or comic strips (Gray 2000) or models, such as dolls, to work through what happened. Emotions are a difficult area for autistic people and a therapist may need to start at a level of examining the six basic emotions. Counselling work is most likely to be individual, child-centred and trauma-focused. Cognitive behavioural therapy is an effective therapeutic approach in autism and sexual abuse. The length of counselling varies, but it appears that many children can recover, at least in part, if they receive appropriate support.

Ways of Preventing Abuse

In terms of prevention, parents need to teach their children the difference between 'good' secrets, which are not kept for long, and 'bad' secrets, which they are supposed never to disclose to anyone. An example of the former might be a surprise for a birthday, whereas the latter might come with a threat to harm our children. We can describe these as 'OK' and 'not OK' secrets.

Additionally, these children should be taught the names of body parts of the opposite gender. Research has found this was lacking in many people with learning difficulties, even if they knew the names of their own private body parts (Hollomotz 2011). Furthermore, severely autistic children should be aware of a range of sexual acts. This is important for them to be able to accurately describe what has happened if sexual abuse occurs.

One of the primary ways of diminishing the potential for sexual abuse is to prevent isolation of autistic children. The fewer people in their social contacts, the greater the risk of sexual abuse, because offenders recognise that their actions are less likely to be reported by their victims (this is one of the reasons for choosing these individuals) and the pool of possible 'reporters' is small. As Hollomotz (2011) said in her exposition of sexual vulnerability and learning difficulties: 'The more friends, family members and helpers who are prepared to be attentive…and are present in the micro and exosystem, the higher the likelihood that violence can be detected and stopped' (Hollomotz 2011, p.46).

CHAPTER 7

THE LONG-TERM FUTURE

This final chapter considers the future. I examine how education and social care settings enable or disable children to learn about sexual issues as they continue to develop. Underlying philosophies and financial pressures can impact on the service that severely autistic children receive from staff. Parents' input and exchange of information with these settings is critical in supporting their children's development, yet there are no consistently applied channels for this. Where their children are able to voice their needs and concerns, there are often external barriers to their being heard, which are not based on their difficulties with communication but on attitudes.

Ultimately, sexuality is a fundamental right for all humans, regardless of intellectual ability. If parents ignore their children's sexual issues, parents invite long-term, intractable problems that can adversely impact on their integration with any community, even that of a social care setting. By embracing their sexuality proactively, parents enhance their children's lives and enable them to reach their fullest potential.

CHALLENGES TO SEXUALITY TEACHING IN SCHOOLS

Attitudes and Beliefs

The belief systems of those closest to their children, including parents, teachers and caregivers, directly influence the quality of sexuality teaching. This includes moral values, which are likely to be more pronounced in church schools. Issues such as homosexuality, relationships and pregnancy may not be covered if staff believe the myth that severely autistic children and adults, like all those with intellectual disabilities, are asexual or childlike, a risk to non-disabled people or vulnerable to abuse.

The Nature of Sexuality Teaching

Sex education for mainstream children is delivered as a standard, generic programme. This is necessary in order to achieve all that needs to be fitted into the personal, social and health education curriculum and on the understanding that much of a non-spectrum child's sexual knowledge is derived from peers and in social situations.

All research points to individualised programmes of sexuality teaching as being essential for people with any form of intellectual disability (Kaeser 1996). Severely autistic children inherently lack social skills and awareness to absorb learning about sexuality from peers, who are likely to be equally socially deficient. Therefore, these children need explicit teaching, which is based on their individual communication, cognitive and developmental levels, and personal needs.

The private nature of sexuality and legal restrictions mean that the effectiveness of teaching is hard to evaluate and the subject is difficult to teach. For example, it is impossible to assess the impact of teaching about masturbation, which may be a necessary area of learning for an individual child. A teacher may use materials to show a scenario of how to masturbate and understand what happens when a young man ejaculates and how to clean up afterwards. But a teacher cannot do hand-over-hand teaching and cannot observe to ascertain if climax has been reached, which might happen with other practical learning.

Often additional individualised programmes are implemented only when students have shown sexualised behaviours. This may be more comfortable for parents, who feel that their children might become sexualised through the process of education and may have used their parental right to withdraw children from sex education lessons. However, the delay in explicit sexuality teaching may create more difficulties as their children have not been prepared for physical changes, or gained even a rudimentary understanding of emotions or sexual arousal, all of which can provoke extreme anxiety because their children will be unable to control what is happening.

Present Provision

There is a perceived lack of availability of suitable sex education materials (Howard-Barr *et al.* 2005). Available resources should be visual and follow current guidance, for example Department for Education and Employment (2000) and OFSTED (2006) in the UK. Even so, some resources have to be adapted for individuals. For example, in Tissot's (2009) research, some students engaged with stick figures in resources using Widgit Rebus symbols, but there was not a picture with an anatomically correct erection. This meant that staff had to create picture jigs to use in a comic strip explaining the stages in masturbation to reach climax (Gray 2000). This study also criticised current resources for being too colourful, distracting or containing too much text (Tissot 2009).

Sexuality teaching which does address autistic students typically focuses on higher functioning individuals (Tarnai and Wolfe 2008). Although some of the literature and research around that end of the autism spectrum may give helpful insights, severely autistic students present with many different sexual and social learning needs which can impact on their daily lives. As an example, some severely autistic students who cannot masturbate to climax may become frustrated and have challenging behaviours, necessitating this as an area for teaching input (Cambridge, Carnaby and McCarthy 2003).

PROACTIVE SEXUALITY TEACHING IN SCHOOLS

Whatever programme of education is delivered should incorporate the following areas.

Baseline Assessment of Sexuality Teaching Needs

Research in Australia suggests that before any teaching of sexual skills is undertaken, a severely autistic person should undergo a functional behaviour assessment. This would involve a whole team approach including parents and would examine the current level of individual communication skills, strengths and specific behaviours (Sterling-Turner and Jordan 2007).

Parents may be requested to keep a diary of any challenging behaviours to try to identify their function for individuals. This includes a definition of the behaviour noting specifics such as frequency and precise detail of behaviours. The aim will be prevention or reduction in harm caused using uniform approaches at home and in school. Proactive plans are a daily plan of prevention of challenging behaviours, which are informed by the functional assessment and should be implemented consistently.

Team Approach

Sexuality teaching should be delivered using a team approach, involving teaching staff, parents and support services, such as speech and language therapists, who should shape education programmes. This should include roles and responsibilities and time provided to allow the team to work together to synchronise the approach. This should be formally documented in an individual education programme (IEP), which will be regularly reviewed. The IEP should reflect the individual's specific needs.

This is the theory. In practice, IEPs may take place without reference to parents, save asking for a signature to confirm that parents have seen and agree with it. This is probably a reflection of time constraints and workload on schools, rather than an explicit desire to exclude parental input. Furthermore, IEPs may not contain any element of sexuality teaching in their aims, focusing instead on academic and daily living skills.

Research shows that many parents feel that professionals should play a larger part in sexuality education, including school and community nurses entering schools as part of PSHE or social workers. Parents' perceptions were that this was not happening and that a pool of professionals participating in conveying information prevented one person having to take responsibility. Ultimately the onus fell on parents (Garbutt 2008).

One advantage of a team approach is that students are less likely to associate a specific person, setting or classroom with sexuality and its teaching. This could become problematic, for instance if students felt that they had a relationship with particular members of staff, resulting in interventions which otherwise might not be necessary.

Input from the Individual

Each student should be involved in the development of their sexuality education programme, giving each a sense of ownership and ensuring that the individual education programme accurately mirrors their children's needs and goals. In addition, the process of being involved is empowering, fosters personal investment in the teaching programme and therefore encourages willingness to learn. If their severely autistic children are regarded as asexual or childlike, their input may not be expected or encouraged, effectively rendering them voiceless in one of the most important areas of life skills (Lesseliers and Van Hove 2002).

In the cases of their severely autistic children, many will not be able to consent to sexuality teaching or have any input into their individual programme. Some research has suggested that professionals make an assessment as to whether or not an individual demonstrates a need for sexuality teaching (Patti 1995). I would argue that waiting for their children to show explicit signs of sexualised behaviours is leaving it too late in their learning careers. By that stage, sexual problem may have become established and will be more difficult to resolve, especially if the child has no foundations for sexuality teaching.

STAFF TRAINING FOR TEACHERS AND PAID CAREGIVERS

Some of the issues to cover include the following:

- The meaning of sexuality, where the group discusses the complex nature of sexuality as it changes through the lifespan and is affected by culture, biology and gender. Sexuality is a broadly defined concept and exists throughout the life cycle.

- Common myths about people who are severely autistic.

- Specific sexuality issues for severely autistic people, such as medication that may affect sexual function.

- Methods of communicating information and sexual health messages, which are individualised and person centred.

- Legal and ethical issues, such as informed consent.

- Specialised referral and further information.

- Teachers and caregivers will need support and training about repetitive behaviours and how to manage behaviours in class or public places, so they are appropriate for the wider world.

Liaising with Parents

It is argued that parents have the designated role of providing explicit sexual information in any collaborative process which reflects the family's religious, cultural and other beliefs. The school has the responsibility for teaching social development for both school and broader community settings (Travers and Tincani 2010). However, many parents feel that they are left with total responsibility for teaching their offspring about all issues around sex (Garbutt 2008). Sexuality education, by its nature, is a sensitive subject and some parents may be unwilling to participate at any level in shaping its teaching and delivery of the topic. If this is the case, commentators still promote incorporating the family's belief system into the IEP (Vaughn *et al.* 2005).

Often, providing clear and regular information to parents will alleviate concerns and demonstrate that what might be deemed 'sexuality education' in the younger years actually is teaching basic building blocks, such as improving communication skills and turn-taking, which are vital for many aspects of future life. Studies outline that many parents want information given early, around the ninth or tenth year of age, but at a level that is appropriate for that child's understanding and cognitive abilities (Tissot 2009).

Developing a series of regular meetings or assemblies about sexuality for parents, caregivers or other family members will ensure that the family gives a uniform and supportive approach to sexuality with severely autistic children. In addition, these consultations will identify barriers and concerns and potential obstacles. Some parents may feel that sexuality of any sort is inappropriate and/or will promote their children's interest in sexual activities. Schools need to work carefully to educate and inform parents to ensure the most constructive outcome for the children under their care.

It is of key importance that parents are made aware of where documented information is available to them to support teaching in school. Schools need to adopt visual approaches to teaching sexuality to severely autistic children. This should be in conjunction with parents, who need and will want to know what their children are being taught. The most useful way of approaching this would be to adopt a sexuality pack of consistent information which could be used in school and was transferable to the home as well. Research identifies that what parents want is information in plain language with clear, explicit pictures or diagrams and a bit of wit thrown in (Garbutt 2008).

It is also important that parents are aware of the possible consequences of not adequately educating their children about sexuality, such as future involvement of their children with the legal system and their increased vulnerability to sex abuse.

The periods of life between primary and secondary education, and on to longer term placements such as day care centres, are referred to as 'transitions'. For parents this is often a distressing time when services are believed to dwindle as children grow older and there is a perception of lack of information and other support. Working with parents reduces the likelihood of conflict and confrontation with the school and gives parents an investment in the teaching process for a subject that will directly affect their family's lives in future.

An Example of Good Practice

Loyne Specialist School, Lancaster, UK introduced a programme for students who have severe learning disabilities. A team approach was used, involving parents and exploring how staff felt and putting in strategies to support them. This was particularly important because staff were to work in close physical proximity to students. One of the stated aims was to reduce challenging behaviours and lessen anxieties in students. The programme incorporated the following aspects:

- Squeezing small balls, which is designed to reduce stress levels by using deep pressure to increase body awareness and proprioceptive input. Proprioception is the dovetailing of tendons, ligaments, muscles and joints to enable fluid movement in the body and the ability of the person to monitor where their body is, for example, when sitting upright.

- Relationship play work, where students rock back to back, which increases trust, builds relationships and facilitates awareness of their own body moving in space.

- Intensive interaction to music, when students are in control of the pacing and shape of movement.

The programme was deliberately slower paced to provide staff the opportunity to closely see even small reactions in students, such as eye contact, or manoeuvring their position ready for firm pressure.

Staff agreed on an optimum time of 20 minutes per session, using bouncing balls prior to the intensive session. There was also a use of repetitious, simple lyrics to extend communication skills. Each session ended with relaxation when students and staff member lie alongside.

The programme was established at four times per week for groups of around eleven students and their staff partners. It was piloted with parents and families, who gave positive feedback.

Careful evaluation after each session has shown that children respond positively across behaviours in school and home. Even students with the most challenging behaviours have shown marked levels of calmness and focus during and after the sessions (Bradbury 2012). This type of work is also helpful for building individual self-esteem and relationships, thus being one of the building blocks of future sexuality teaching.

Communicating Information

Most severely autistic children will respond well to visual learning tools, using systems such as TEACCH2 or Picture Exchange Communication System (PECS) (Baker 2000). Social stories are one of the most useful ways of depicting what is said and thought in situations and help the children examine the consequences of what they might do (Tarnai and Wolfe 2008). Care should be taken with visual teaching strategies which, if taken out of context, may mean that teaching messages are misinterpreted or misunderstood (Tissot 2009). This is particularly the case with sexual behaviours so, for example, liaising with parents might yield photographs of children's bedrooms, which will accurately show children where they can masturbate. This gives precise information for visual learning.

The great advantage that schools have is the ability to get children to work in groups, acting out what might happen in life and what to say or do should certain situations arise, with an emphasis on social integration (Attwood 2000, 2006). Role-play can help flesh out sexuality teaching but this should be reinforced at regular intervals in different contexts for the health messages to be understood. Even in severely autistic children, group work can be effective at the very least, in learning turn-taking and just being with others. In general, schools will play a significant part in developing children's communication skills, how they convey information and receive it and how to develop and maintain friendships. All of these factors are essential in teaching about sexuality.

Content of Teaching Programmes

Teaching programmes should be proactive and not wait for their children to demonstrate sexualised behaviours before a programme of sexuality teaching starts. Lessons should be developed along the lines of 'building blocks' or incremental teaching, including friendships and other relationships, which can be explored and built. Children with severe autism should be taught early in their school career about self-care and safety activities, which form the basic foundations on which to build sexuality education. However, continuous work on improving communication skills, social skills, such as turn-taking and appropriate greetings, and play skills are fundamental to enabling their children to effectively learn about sexuality. Regardless of their age or level of development, research shows that their children should have social skills training (Koller 2000). As Hatton and Tector (2010, p.72) put it: 'building blocks…are essential parts in the development of social competency and it is within social competency that their understanding of sexuality and relationships must lie.'

As children become more socially developed, teaching will focus on how to build relationships, whether these are friendships or more intimate. Lessons could examine how to find and share common interests, which could start from the point of sharing a computer using turn-taking skills and being interested in the computer work of their partner, even if this is limited to pointing, using single words and jumping. These may not be refined ways of communicating but they do denote shared interest and, if carefully supported by teaching staff, can lead to greater verbal expressions.

Sexuality teaching will also cover emotions in children themselves and others and how to express feelings such as anger and sadness. Managing rejection and how to express love and affection are important areas of learning. The advantage of this kind of work in schools is that it can take place in groups, which give a dynamic that cannot be achieved in the home setting.

Schools should provide the minimum basics of anatomy, physiology and safety (Gill and Hough 2007). However, throughout this book I have argued that these simply are not enough to equip their children with the necessary knowledge and skills for sexuality. At the simplest of levels, engaging in the wider community can become impossible or very limited if students cannot make a distinction between private and public behaviours. There is an intellectual argument for their children to be educated with a focus on masturbation and creating sexuality based on solo activities (Cambridge *et al.* 2003). For some of their children this is where their sexual expression may lie for the totality of their future. For others, they may develop their sexuality further and they have a right to the knowledge and skills around issues such as sexual intercourse, sexually transmitted infections and pregnancy.

POLICIES AND PROCEDURES IN SCHOOLS

Policies should cover sexual activity on school grounds. If the school is residential, care staff should allow privacy in bedrooms at regular times to allow masturbation. If it is a day school, masturbation should be prevented from happening at all in school. I have personal experience of parents who feel that teachers should allow masturbation in lavatories with the cubicle (stall) locked. The parents would argue that this behaviour is conducive to the rules around public and private activities, it being a 'private behaviour in a private place'. These parents also expressed a desire that their children understood that masturbation was 'OK'. Certainly, non-spectrum adults will masturbate in lavatories. However, parents have to give their autistic children fast rules because they do not have the capacity to differentiate between circumstances. For example, if they masturbate in school lavatories, they will not perceive a difference with other lavatories, which makes them vulnerable to being approached for other sexual acts in public lavatories or being arrested for lewd acts in a public place. Their children may always be accompanied at present, but parents have to consider how they will be in twenty years' time, for example, when parents may not be around to guard public lavatories to ensure they are safe.

Induction training and ongoing training around sexuality should be available for teaching staff. This should be regularly reviewed in the light of changing government policy and issues that might arise in school. The purpose of staff training is to enable teaching staff to create a firm basis for the building blocks of more complex issues relating to sexuality including relationships and social competence.

In addition, staff training should allow staff to explore their own beliefs and attitudes towards sexuality and how it impacts on their abilities to teach the subject. This includes teaching staff at primary and middle school levels where the foundations of more complex teaching are laid. Research suggests that several characteristics are needed for a professional to provide optimal sexuality education (Fegan, Rauch and McCarthy 1993):

- objectivity

- confidence in the subject

- openness and directness

- awareness of their own attitudes to minimise bias

- knowledge of current information available and accurate delivery of it

- clearly and frequently communicating with and listening to parents

- asking for advice from 'experts' as necessary

- using repetition, reinforcement and generalising information to underpin sexuality teaching

- using multisensory teaching methods, largely visual, such as drawings and models.

Schools should develop and implement strategies to support staff, parents and other involved people. This might involve procedures around same-gender staff accompanying children to the lavatory if they need personal care, for example, or when sexualised behaviours are directed towards staff or other students. This may require the involvement of other professionals as consultants, such as when medical doctors' opinions are sought for sexualised behaviours or educational psychologists are asked for advice about conveying specific messages about sexuality.

At a policy level, there should be regular reviews of sexuality teaching materials and current implementation of school personal, social and health education (PSHE), which includes sexuality, across the curriculum. This will be guided by latest government policy, any local government input or training and/or voluntary input. However, there are few resources that are suitable for the severe end of the autism spectrum (Grieve *et al.* 2006). Implementation of sexuality training should be evaluated and reviewed regularly.

Schools may need to consider same-sex teachers, depending on the responses of students (Realmuto and Ruble 1999). Cultural factors may mean that parents want their children taught according to their gender, that is, boys with boys and girls with girls. This can be problematic in smaller institutions so some schools favour students who are perceived to be 'nonsexual' (Allen 2007). It also presents difficulties in special schools, which tend to be overwhelmingly staffed by females. Codes of practice are written in gender-neutral language which gives little guidance about gender issues, so this must be dealt with at a local (school) level.

Teachers need to be aware of supportive interventions to help students transition into supported living or social care settings. This is a specialised need and is not covered by generic personal, social and health education guidelines.

Policy should include developing a referral system for individual students to programmes of support and specialist consultation if necessary, such as medical support.

LEGAL ASPECTS OF SEXUALITY TEACHING

The personal, social and health education component of the National Curriculum in the UK requires that sexuality is taught (Department for Education and Skills 2002) but restrictions under the Children and Young Persons Act 2006 mean that legally teachers are unable to effectively monitor aspects of sexuality and safety messages with this group and measure effectiveness of teaching (Van Bourgondien, Reichle and Palmer 1997).

In residential schools students are prohibited from consenting to sexualised behaviours with another person under the Sexual Offences Act 2003. The Children and Young Persons Act 2006 supports the need for enabling students to explore their sexuality in consideration of their limited abilities and the law. This Act also provides for a safeguarding children representative to be involved when teaching is, of necessity, graphic, for example masturbation. This protects the child in question and members of staff.

SEXUALISED BEHAVIOURS

It is difficult to address sexualised behaviours which happen in public because:

- They provide instant gratification, which may be reinforced by the response of teachers, caregivers or parents and rapidly become a repetitive behaviour.

- Staff and parents prefer not to teach about sexualised behaviours so there are often no established programmes of support for students.

Once the link is made between stimulations and touching the genital area, this can be difficult to break. Other reinforcements may not be as strong or immediate in impact on the individual, who may be very opportunistic. If this happens in public, it becomes a duty of care issue to be addressed urgently but staff may not be skilled up to manage it. If not dealt with effectively or efficiently, the issue is likely to become more significant.

Learning Outcomes that Students with Severe Autism Want

The following text is adapted from Tissot (2009):

- input into how they are supported by staff in developing sexuality

- rights and responsibilities

- resolving issues

- opportunities to meet people

- information and resources they can access

- future training and group work for students.

RESIDENTIAL INSTITUTIONS

Severely autistic children may enter residential institutions, either as full-time students, where they may return to the family home at weekends or holidays, or as an adult placement. In the latter, they would reside permanently at an institution. An alternative to this might be small units of supervised housing in the community.

The Children and Young Persons Act 2006 prevents sexual activity between students in residential schools, regardless if this is consensual. In residential schools, if residents appear to be attracted to each other, staff may try the following:

- Assessing if the developing situation is consensual, if there are power issues and who initiates the contact.

- Discussing the issue as a team and considering strategies, involving parents and the residents.

- Accompanying them to do non-sexual activities together.

- Keeping parents informed of the situation.

- Ensuring that residents are not left unsupervised in each other's bedrooms.

Liaising with parents is essential to supporting their children in issues around sexuality. Tissot (2009) gives an example of a male student at a residential school who had difficulty masturbating to climax, which was causing him to injure his genitals. The school worked with his parents, using the same support materials in the form of instruction books to guide the young man through the process of successful masturbation. The local safeguarding children representative was involved and examined the proposed reading material, in accordance with the Children and Young Persons Act 2006, which also dictated that no staff could observe the young man to instruct or help him in person. It took over three months to resolve the issue and enable the young man to reach climax.

Often placements take place after home breakdown due to exhaustion, marital rift, a death or incident at home. Sometimes they happen because parents cannot manage their children's behaviours, especially around aggression and sexuality. This is potentially problematic because staff at residential institutions will inherit established challenging behaviours, which they will have to unpick and manage. This could include extensive re-education about sexual issues.

Statutory guidance on sex education gives parents the right to withdraw their children from sexuality teaching. Both in residential and day schools it is clearly essential to forge positive relationships with parents to gain their support for educating their children about sex issues. Parents need to understand the limitations that lack of sex education could have on their children's ability to integrate into their local community. Some sexualised behaviours might mean they could effectively be incarcerated and permitted into the public domain only with strict limits and monitoring.

Regardless of the scenario which led to the placement, parents should be encouraged to maintain close links with their children. This would include regular visits and the possibility of visits to the family home. The placement, therefore, should be in close proximity to the family. This was a patent concern in the case of Winterbourne View in the UK where adults with severe learning difficulties, including autism, were placed at a considerable distance from their families, sometimes as far as 200 miles away. This limited the numbers of family and friends visiting and regularity of visits, allowing appalling long-term physical and emotional abuse to fester and not be recognised.

Visits from Family and Friends

Visits from family and friends have several functions: first, their children need the stability of knowing they have family which is separate to other residents, that is 'theirs' and part of their identity. Relationships with family members should not be destroyed by children living in placements. Parents can act as a vital link to the community and parents should not assume their children will remain in institutions, which should be few in their society. The movement in community care has been towards small, supported living for severely autistic children since the 1990s.

Second, visits can be impromptu if relatives live nearby, creating an environment where staff who are unsuitable for the job are more likely to be identified sooner.

Third, lack of management and leadership, flagged up as a problem in Winterbourne View, is likely to be spotted, documented and reported back to senior management.

After residential school, children may have an adult placement. At this point it is important to retain any friendships that have been forged in school. This is likely to fall to parents to facilitate and encourage.

PAID CAREGIVERS AND GENDER ISSUES

Research has found clear differences between perceptions of caring roles of male and female caregivers (Wilson *et al.* 2009). Female caregivers had real concerns about physicality and possible aggression from male clients. This inhibited their abilities to give care as they would to female clients, which allows for relational closeness with clients, not as sexual partners but as conduits for confidences and questions about relationships and intimacy. Males were viewed as potentially problematic and threatening.

However, females were essential in caring environments to foster positive outcomes for male health, male sexual health, male expression, male physicality and male interaction. I would argue this is partly because women act as role models of how females in society behave, so male clients observe how male staff interact with female members of staff. Females also give their male children a balance which is reflective of wider society and enables them to function better in the social world.

Male caregivers tend to focus on activities as the basis of their relationships with clients. They are more relaxed with sexual issues in relation to male clients and will advocate for male clients if they perceive themselves to be trusted in their role as caregiver by that client. Unlike women, male caregivers retreat from relational proximity, whether physical or emotional, due to a fear of being accused of inappropriate behaviour (Wilson *et al.* 2009).

Some research has suggested that males with severe autism and other intellectual disabilities are generally viewed negatively as a source of aggression and sexual deviance. The study proposed that male staff were vital to reversing this impression and the following measures should be implemented:

- More men to be employed as caregivers to act as positive role models. Police and employment checks should weed out inappropriate candidates.

- Male clients should have access to male health workers.

- More training around sexuality and men for staff and group work for residents.

- A focus on positive expressions of their physicality, such as sporting activities.

- An emphasis on developing residential placements into male-friendly environments.

- To accommodate cultural issues, men should be taught separately by a male.

Sexual health should be part of every person-centred care plan, review and future planning. The Family Planning Association of Belfast suggests that there should be a nominated member of staff available to clients who may want to discuss an aspect of sexuality. The difficulty that may arise from this is the danger that their severely autistic children may start to associate that person with all aspects of sex and even develop in their minds sexual feelings for that member of staff (FPA and Public Health Agency 2010; Tissot 2009). There should be sexuality initiatives in day centres, including appropriate behaviours and self-protection.

Social Care Association (SCA undated) in the UK states the values under which staff work should be explicit:

- Staff should ensure that service users are enabled to assert their individuality and rights in group living.

- Service users have a right to complain or comment on the service they receive.

- Staff should incorporate sexuality and relationships as part of the overall care plan for service users.

POLICIES IN SOCIAL CARE

As with other services, social care exists within a series of policies and procedures, which are designed to protect clients and service providers. Clear policies support staff and reflect the philosophy of the service itself. Policies should not be theoretical tomes but should act as a framework within which staff safely can work. Procedures should enable frontline staff by giving them the knowledge of how to implement principles identified in policy.

Historically social care has moved towards incorporating clients into the process of decision-making. This, in turn, maximises the possibilities for their taking responsibility and exercising choice. This can be achieved only with the willingness of management to establish a dialogue with clients and create robust policies and procedures to ensure clients' rights are maintained.

Recruitment

Social care managers can be explicit in the advertisements for new staff, specifying desirable attitudes and key values necessary to support clients' sexuality. Training strategies should include ongoing supervision and support and sexuality and relationships should be in all training for all levels of staff. Some reports even suggest that clients should be involved in the recruitment process, such as pinpointing appropriate attitudes in practitioners.

While this is an ideal, in practice frontline staff complain of feeling under pressure by social care management to 'contain' clients rather than create an environment of supported sexual expression and sexuality in a homely setting (Tissot 2009). Research has found that attitudes in terms of sexuality are inconsistent, ranging from preventing all sexual contact whatsoever (including hand-holding and cuddling) to formally checking with both parties that they were able to give consent to sexual intercourse and there were no power issues attached to that consent (SCA undated). Most caregivers in research (FPA and Public Health Agency 2010) thought that staff should stop sexual acts such as sexual intercourse and masturbating but allow hand-holding and kissing. Whatever the approach, it varied further if the attraction were same sex, once again giving a mixed message to clients.

One candid piece of research identified that sex in lavatories at day centres and social clubs for people with learning disabilities was relatively common (SCA undated). The author of the report felt that this was due to situations where even the mildest form of sexual contact was prohibited, so sex became secretive (in lavatories), which renders people more vulnerable to sexual abuse and sexual exploitation. The same research urged that those clients who have the capacity to consent to sex be given rights to have overnight guests and double beds and not have obstacles erected to prevent developing sexual relationships (SCA undated).

Ongoing Work

Social care staff should receive ongoing supervision in order to work effectively. Supervision in this sense means the offloading of counselling and other support issues onto a supervisor or counsellor, rather than necessarily being physically observed. Teamwork offers support for staff, as does consistent in-service training to develop ideas and discuss issues. In sexuality, this could mean the need to have a multiagency approach to resolve problems, such as sexualised behaviours. However, this does not appear to happen often enough in practice.

Involvement of Clients and Parents

The Sex and Relationships research project used a series of drama workshops to explore the views and experiences of those with learning difficulties and gave them a voice (Garbutt 2008). This may be difficult with many severely autistic children, but using pictures and models may enable them to communicate issues, for example difficulties achieving a climax, wanting more time and privacy to masturbate or wanting to use sexual aids (toys).

If parents still have parental rights over their adult offspring, they should be involved in the development of processes to support them. This may be in relation to friendships or other relationships that may be created in community living or the procedure that happens if their children act sexually inappropriately in public, for example. Input from parents should be used in formalised care plans, to which staff will refer.

CONSENT

The Sexual Offences Act 2003 determines what is and is not acceptable. The age of consent in the UK is 16 regardless of the genders of the people involved. As parents, it is useful to know the criteria that will be used when social care staff assess consent in relation to their adult children. The following are fundamental to assessing capacity to consent, when an individual should have an awareness and understanding of:

- the mechanics of a specific sexual act (consent being act specific)

- the potential health risks that may result from sexual acts, such as sexually transmitted infections

- the fact that sexual intercourse between a man and a woman may result in pregnancy.

The British Institute of Learning Disabilities (BILD) developed the Capacity Assessment Tool to assist professionals involved in making decisions about whether or not a client can consent to sexual acts. It details areas which should be covered in assessing individuals and is a resource for facilitating communication using pictures (see Resources). It also covers issues such as power relations and assertion skills in sexual relationships.

Probably the greatest issue around sexuality and the law is that it is not prescriptive, but leaves social care management to interpret legislation. This interpretation, of course, will reflect attitudes and opinions of management and frontline staff and could go some way to explaining why service provision and support for clients is so variable.

GOALS OF INPUT INTO
SEXUALITY IN SOCIAL CARE

Again, these rely on working closely with schools from whom clients 'graduate' from being students. The ideal would be an extension of social skills and knowledge learned in school, which requires an acceptance that children will continue to develop and a willingness to embrace and work with that.

Programmes of sexuality learning should continue and should be based on a functional assessment of behaviours to identify individual learning needs. Placements in institutions or small community settings are times when their children will become exposed to greater sexual issues. For example, this may be the first time that they have shared an accommodation with anyone other than family members, so their children may become sexually attracted and attractive to other people. These experiences can be built upon and their children can be guided and supported if social care staff have appropriate attitudes and skills which underpin the development of their children into valued members of society, complete with their sexuality. Positive sexuality policies and teaching will support their children to engage more fully in living, with less likelihood of their being abused or exploited sexually.

Research has shown a real difference between the sexual knowledge and skills base of older people with learning difficulties compared with those who have been educated using the National Curriculum (Hollomotz 2011). Older clients have less knowledge and fewer skills because many of them were excluded from sex education in school (Shakespeare *et al.* 1996). In effect, this means that these cohorts of clients still need sexuality teaching and many will be living in social care settings. Some innovative projects, such as women's and men's health groups in day care centres, have been successful in outreaching information about sexual health. In addition, social groups based on shared interests enable clients to experience developing friendships. Social care staff are effectively 'gatekeepers' to one of the most important aspects of the lives of their clients, that of building and maintaining friendships. But these pieces of work require proactive management approaches, in-service training for staff and support to maintain standards. At present, this type of service is patchy and may not be a priority in times of austerity. Yet the long-term benefits to the individual and society are immense.

FAMILY INPUT

Parental belief systems undoubtedly have a profound effect on the experiences of their severely autistic children. This also affected their children's sexual rights, often negatively (Johnson *et al.* 2002). Despite many parents wanting their children to share the same rights in terms of sexuality as non-spectrum people, their deep fears about safety and perceived vulnerability of their offspring often supersede this impulse (Simpson, Lafferty and McConkey 2006).

OBTAINING INFORMATION

Some parents find that they are forced to fight for even basic information around sexuality, in similarity to other areas of support for their children. Sometimes this is achieved via the family doctor. Depending on the school, information can be made available from teaching staff. However, this is variable and studies have identified that many parents claim to have no concept of what is being taught about sexuality in their children's school and no consultation process has happened (Garbutt 2008).

Parents want schools to adopt a proactive approach, organising regular meetings with them and issuing information. This would be something in the region of one meeting per season (autumn/fall, spring and summer) as a basic strategy for regularity. Additionally, parents suggest it would be useful to have contact numbers for key professionals who might give advice about sexual issues (Garbutt 2008). Certainly from my experience, parents use autism websites to ask incisive questions about sexuality and their children, but it is clear that problems are often well established and the answers of dubious or variable value, which would suggest experienced professionals might be more pertinent.

The value of informal meetings with other parents to discuss sexuality was cited in research as giving individuals confidence and a source of advice. Some parents felt that this type of meeting happened automatically at special schools but was less likely at mainstream schools. However, it is clear when one examines this issue that it is often the willingness of the school management (the head teacher and governors in the UK) to engage families and the wider community, that dictates if any involvement happens. This is regardless of it being a special or a mainstream school. It is certainly a feature that is worthwhile looking for in a school's prospectus or enquiring about when selecting schools.

Due to some social misconceptions about special needs children and educational establishments, special schools frequently try to liaise and communicate broadly to ensure community support. One could argue that schools which behave in this way are more likely to facilitate the integration of students into the wider community. One of the most fundamentally important aspects of doing so is to establish the difference between acceptable and unacceptable public behaviours, largely centred on dangerous, aggressive or sexualised acts. For this reason, many community-focused schools are also well versed in sexuality teaching, both in knowledge and skills.

The National Autistic Society (NAS) in the UK and similar organisations in other countries provide a source of information and a means of uniting with other parents of children with autism. Local groups meet on a regular basis and can be a basis for sharing advice and thoughts or problems about sexuality either at meetings or on websites such as Facebook NAS pages. Social networking sites certainly provide an arena for sharing concerns and events, so breaking down the isolation that is so prevalent in parenting in autism.

CO-DEPENDENCY

As parents become older and less able, co-dependency can develop between them and their severely autistic offspring. This is when the parents become dependent on their autistic children for care and support in a way that is not emotionally healthy. Depending on how socially developed the child, who will be an adult by this stage, has become, the care may range from food shopping to a level of personal care. The autistic adult effectively is trapped in this social situation, paradoxically like the parent may have felt with the child. From the outside this may seem a reasonable, family decision to reverse care as the primary carer becomes needy. However, the following should be considered:

- This is not a decision reached by the 'child' who, by definition, is unlikely to be able to translate knowledge into daily decision-making.

- Autistic people thrive off routine and find new situations alarming, so they may have been told by the parent that they will have to move and separate unless the 'child' does the caring. The parent may believe this to be the case.

- The parent may not want to have a different situation or have strangers in the form of paid caregivers entering the home to provide them with care. So they rely on their 'child'.

- Relying on the 'child' for care ensures the child remains 'safe' in the home and protected from what many parents regard as a hostile social world for their child. This may be particularly the case if the child has been isolated in the home under the guise of 'protection' for most of his/her life.

- The parent may feel the child 'owes them' for the years of care and lack of personal social or other life the parent has had in order to care for their child.

This may seem a reasonable argument with non-spectrum children, who may step in to support their ageing parents. However, it is different when the 'child' continues to have considerable need for support. The ageing and greater dependence of the parent do not negate the social and support needs of the child.

In effect, the autistic 'child' may become still further isolated, which ultimately will cause them to be more vulnerable in the long-term future when the parent has gone completely.

Parents need to be planning what will happen for their autistic children and how this will be funded. If this involves their children moving into a different environment, parents need to introduce the idea, new supportive people and the actual placement as early as possible for their children to adapt to future change. This can be supported by whatever means of communication their children use. Planning also gives parents peace of mind that when they are gone, their children will be as supported as possible and able to lead a life beyond us.

CONCLUSIONS

In the UK, the movement towards inclusion of even moderately autistic children into mainstream schools means that non-specialist teaching staff may have to address issues around sexuality with these children. Special educational needs coordinators (SENCOs) will take the lead in provision of appropriate sexual health education.

A key difficulty in severely autistic children learning about sexuality is that their parents are often exhausted, have little or no respite from caring duties and feel they are left with the responsibility for teaching sexuality, which may not even seem like an essential to them. Many parents feel that they are inviting their children to become sexualised by broaching the subject. They discover rather late that tackling this area of learning is best done in childhood rather than waiting for sexualised behaviours to appear in young adulthood.

Teaching and residential caregivers may feel that teaching about sexuality and supporting their autistic students and clients is not their job, especially as this is an emotive subject. Again, it is only when presented with sexualised behaviours in public or directed towards staff, for example, that these health educators start to tackle the subject of sexuality.

With parents, teaching staff and caregivers, the approach to sexuality is too often reactionary. A proactive approach would be more likely to succeed in preventing entrenching, inappropriate sexual behaviours, which could cause autistic adults to become embroiled in the legal system or, at the very least, prevent them from assimilating as far as possible into society.

Looking forward, schools should foster relationships with parents at the first instance from primary to the end of secondary schools, regardless of whether or not the school is special or mainstream, day or residential. Despite their motivations being to support and educate severely autistic children, schools and parents often have differing philosophies and pressures. Education tends to be driven by performance indicators such as academy status or OFSTED reports. Parents tend to be driven by emotions and exhaustion. Parents too often feel that schools do not understand their position and there may be a need for mediation to reach agreement and advocacy for parents and, if they can participate in IEPs, for children. Undoubtedly, the interface between schools and parents is an area ripe for study and research with a view to developing strategies to improve relations.

Of course, the people most affected by decisions and the practice of sexuality education are severely autistic children. Their voices are all too often ignored or given cursory relevance. For meaningful, holistic actions around sexuality, parents, schools and social care staff need to actively seek the opinions and involvement of these children. It is true that many of their more challenged youngsters will have limited input, but parents need to approach this from the perspective that they will continue to develop, that lack of verbalisation does not necessarily equate with lack of intellect and that to honour their 'right' to sexuality, their children first have a right to influence, if not direct, their learning (Lesselliers 1999).

The most productive way forward would be an explicit, unified approach from parents, teaching staff and other allied professions who attend to their children. A multiagency approach to sexuality teaching could involve any of the following professionals:

- parents
- teaching staff
- special educational needs coordinators
- governors
- speech and language therapists
- occupational therapists
- medical doctors
- educational psychologist
- caregivers in social care and education
- school nurses
- psychiatric team
- other workers such as respite caregivers.

Consistency, clear communication and explicit language are essential to conveying sexual messages in a meaningful way to their children. Yet parents do not practise these key elements when discussing sexuality. Instead, parents ignore sexuality or hope that someone else will take responsibility for it because the area is uncomfortable for so many of us and we lack sufficient information and support.

Ultimately, parents need to learn how to enable their autistic children to develop friendships and make mistakes. Parents need to create a supportive environment which enables relationships and acts as a safety net.

Accepting that their children may never have intimate relationships with another person and/or have children themselves is something many parents may have acknowledged and grieved over in the early years after diagnosis. Accepting that they can still have a fulfilling sexual life (even if this is solo) empowered by knowledge and skills developed with their support is a perspective that some parents may not have thought through.

Severely autistic children may continue to develop socially and cognitively into adulthood. Educational input will remain important for developing social and communication skills well beyond formal school years. The same can be said of sexuality teaching and experience of friendships and other relationships. This continuous process of creating independence to as high a level as is possible, will give their children the best chance of managing without their parents in future.

Some of these children will never be able to translate knowledge into daily decision-making or give consent to sexual acts due to lack of cognitive ability. However, intellectual disability should not prevent their children from exploring their sexuality, which is, after all, an integral part of all humanity. Autistic children will want to explore sexuality and create sexual relationships (Tarnai and Wolfe 2008) but they must exercise their right to sexuality within a framework of social mores and culture (Swango-Wilson 2008). It is a sign of a mature society to embrace all parts of their population into notions of sexuality, with all the excitement, fulfilment and joy it can bring.

Definition of Autism Spectrum Disorder

Diagnosis depends on the patient presenting with symptoms from each of the so-called 'Triad of Impairments' listed below.

Impairment of Social Interaction

- Lack of eye contact or covering their head or eyes persistently.

- Reluctance to cuddle or to be appropriately tactile.

- Inappropriate responses to social interactions, such as laughing at others' injuries.

- Aloofness or indifference to others.

- No spontaneous attempts to make social contact.

- Lack of empathy with others.

- Following their own 'agenda' of (often seemingly odd) activities.

Impairment of Social Communication

- Delay in speech, with no underlying hearing deficit.

- Not responding to his/her name.

- Echoing words or phrases.

- Generally preferring to be alone.

- Difficulty interacting with others.

- Difficulty expressing wants or needs – may use gestures.
- Not understanding the spoken word as a means of conveying or gaining information.
- Inability to interpret body language or the nuances of the spoken word.
- A literal understanding of speech.

Impairment of Social Imagination

- Concentration on the minutia, not the overall picture.
- Inappropriate attachment to objects.
- Prolonged repetitive behaviours.
- Spinning themselves or objects.
- Lining up objects.
- Insistence on (often elaborate) routines.
- Inability to play with toys with any imagination.
- Not mimicking parental behaviours such as vacuuming.
- Displaying tight, repetitive interests, often with vast knowledge of these.

Other Signs

- Over- or under-sensitivity to pain.
- Toe-walking – people with ASD describe feeling pain if they place the entire foot on the floor.
- No fear of danger.
- Aggression or tantrums for no apparent reason.
- Self-injurious behaviours, such as head banging or scratching.
- Hyperactivity.
- Sleep disturbances.

Repetitive, focused behaviours have a purpose, in that they protect the child from what can be a bewildering world, by giving comforting predictability. Distracting the child, blocking or removing the items of focus can cause great distress.

Proprioception

In some children with ASDs, structures such as muscles, tendons, ligaments and joints do not coordinate effectively. This dovetailing of efficient coordination, which includes spatial and body awareness, is referred to as proprioception. In practical terms, this means that children may be unable to sit upright and maintain that position. It can be difficult for a child to sit at a table and problematic for any gross motor activities such as cycling and trampolining.

Other autistic children may need proprioceptive input in order to keep their bodies calm and their arousal levels regulated, so they will stim to achieve this and need regular physical activity.

APPENDIX 3

Epilepsy

Around a quarter of severely autistic children will start to have seizures when they reach adolescence, the onset of which can be indicated by aggression or other unusual behaviours for the child (Edelson 2011). Such seizures are caused by high hormone levels. They can be limited to absences which are a loss of consciousness lasting about ten seconds, characterised by blank staring, then the child returning to task, oblivious to the absence. This seems mild and can go unnoticed, but will seriously impact on the child's ability to follow what is happening in the social world and can lead to great anxiety because events seem sudden and unexpected due to absences. Seizures can be the opposite extreme of a full-body, generalised nature, when the following happens:

- The person drops to the ground in an unconscious state, sometimes letting out a cry.

- The person becomes rigid, often with an arched back.

- The person may stop breathing, so the lips turn blue and the neck and face can turn puffy and red.

- Involuntary contractions of muscles in the body result in the entire body shaking violently. The person's jaw may be clenched and the breathing is noisy. There can be frothing as the mouth releases saliva that may be blood-stained if the person has bitten their tongue or lips.

- The person may lose bladder or bowel control.

- The person's muscles become relaxed and breathing goes back to normal, usually within a few minutes. They may well be dazed, act oddly for them and then fall into a deep sleep.

The obviousness of this type of seizure means that it will be addressed medically without delay. All epileptic seizures can be treated with medication, although sometimes the dose needs to be titrated according to the person's body weight or propensity of the seizures to respond to treatment.

At times, treatment only significantly reduces but cannot wholly prevent seizures, so parents need to know the immediate care of someone who has seizures. This is also useful if we are to actively support our children's friendships, because there is a real chance that their autistic friends will have seizures even if our own children do not.

The immediate care for someone having a full-body, generalised seizure is as follows:

1. Try to minimise the person's injury if you see them falling.

2. Make space around them and remove anything that might cause injury, such as sharp objects or hot drinks.

3. Try to protect the person's head by putting something soft under it, like a jacket or cushion.

4. Loosen clothing around the neck.

5. Time the seizure from dropping to the ground to regaining consciousness.

6. *Do not force anything into the mouth to try to keep the airway open.*

7. *Do not try to restrain the person's movements during the seizure.*

8. *Do not move the person unless they are in immediate danger where they are located.*

The time to call an ambulance is:

• If this is the person's first seizure (check with a child's parents if their child has had seizures).

• If the person is unconscious for more than ten minutes.

• If the seizure lasts for more than five minutes.

• If the person is having repeated seizures.

(St John's Ambulance Service 2013)

Possible New Ideas for Protocols to Assessing Cases of Sexual Abuse

- Introduce the child to the interviewer more than once before the actual interview takes place.

- Locate the interview in a familiar place where the child is likely to feel comfortable. This may depend on where the abuse is thought to have taken place. A school classroom may be appropriate, or the medical consultant's regular office.

- The interviewers need to understand that eye contact not only is unnecessary but also may be extremely uncomfortable for an autistic child. Often doing something else while talking will elicit more information than a direct question and answer session, which many of our children would find frightening and might well cause them to be mute.

- The interviews may have to be in short sessions, allowing many breaks due to our children's short attention spans and creating the opportunity for our children to develop a rapport or at least familiarity with the interviewer.

- Interviewers need to be aware that stimming behaviours will enable the child to keep anxieties suppressed by self-calming. This may mean that the child is in constant motion throughout an interview and important words may be spoken or communication made amid these physical movements.

- Instead of using unfamiliar anatomically correct dolls to enable the child to describe what happened, it may be more fruitful to allow a toy that the child is familiar with into the interview. This may elicit spoken evidence to the toy or the child may demonstrate what happened using familiar toys.

- It may be helpful to have someone who knows the child well to be with them at interview. This probably should not be a family member but a professional, such as a teacher or caregiver, depending on the circumstances.

- Interviewers need to realise that autistic children do not have a clear understanding of body space and body language. These social deficits may otherwise taint the impression of the interviewer of the child's communications.

References

Allen, L. (2007) 'Denying the sexual subject: Schools' regulation of student sexuality.' *British Education Research Journal 33*, 2, 221–234.

Ambitious About Autism (AAA) (2013) *Stats and Facts.* Available at www.ambitiousaboutautism. org.uk/page/about_autism/stats_and_facts/index.cfm (accessed February 2013).

American Psychiatric Association (2000) *Diagnostic and Statistical Manual of Mental Disorders, 4th edition, text revised* (DSM-IV-TR). Washington, DC: American Psychiatric Association.

American Psychological Association (2013) 'Understanding child sexual abuse: Education, prevention and recovery.' Available at www.apa.org/pubs/info/brochures/sex-abuse. aspx?item=4# (accessed April 2013).

Ashkenazy, E. and Yergeau, M. (eds) (2013) *Relationships and Sexuality: A Handbook for and by Autistic People.* Washington: Autistic Self Advocacy Network.

Attwood, T. (2000) 'Strategies for improving the social integration of children with Asperger Syndrome.' *Autism 4*, 1, 85–100.

Attwood, T. (2006) *The Complete Guide to Asperger's Syndrome.* London: Jessica Kingsley Publishers.

Autism Speaks (2013) 'Recognising and preventing sexual abuse.' Available at www.autismspeaks. org/family-services/autism-safety-project/sexual-abuse (accessed April 2013).

Baird, G., Simonoff, E., Pickles, A., Chandler, S., *et al.* (2006) 'Prevalence of disorders of the autism spectrum in a population cohort of children in South Thames: The Special Needs and Autism Project (SNAP).' *The Lancet 368*, 9531, 210–215.

Baker, S. (2000) 'Learning through pictures.' *Communication*, spring, 15–17.

Billstedt, E., Gillberg, I.C. and Gillberg, C. (2005) 'Autism after adolescence: population-based 13- to 22-year follow-up study of 120 individuals with autism diagnosed in childhood.' *Journal of Autism and Development Disorders 35*, 3, 351–360.

Biro, F.M. and Dorn, L.D. (2006) 'Puberty and adolescent sexuality.' *Psychiatric Annals 36*, 1, 685–690.

Borland, S. (2012) 'Care centres to be closed after abuse scandal as minister says there must be complete culture change in treatment.' *Mail Online*, 11 December 2012. Available at www.dailymail.co.uk/news/article-2246197/Care-centres-closed-Winterbourne-View-abuse-scandal.html (accessed June 2013).

Bradbury, B. (2012) 'The pressure principal.' *SEN Special Educational Needs Magazine.* Available at www.senmagazine.co.uk/articles/1012-how-a-body-awareness-programme-can-aid-relaxation-and-promote-learning-for-children-with-asd (accessed June 2013).

Burn, M.F. and Brown, S. (2006) 'A review of the cognitive distortions in child sex offenders: An examination of the motivations and mechanisms that underlie the justification for abuse.' *Aggression and Violent Behavior 11*, 3, 225–236.

Burton-Smith, R., McVilly, K., Yazbeck, M., Parmenter, T. and Tsutsui, T. (2009) 'Service and support needs of Australian carers supporting a family member with disability at home.' *Journal of Intellectual and Developmental Disability 34*, 3, 239–247.

Cambridge, P., Carnaby, S. and McCarthy, M. (2003) 'Responding to masturbation in supporting sexuality and challenging behaviour in services for people with learning disabilities.' *Journal of Learning Disabilities 7*, 3, 251–266.

Cavanagh Johnson, T. (1999) *Understanding Your Child's Sexual Behavior: What's Natural and Healthy.* Oakland, CA: New Harbinger.

Cavanagh Johnson, T. (2002) 'Some considerations about sexual abuse and children with sexual behavior problems.' *Journal of Trauma and Dissociation 3*, 4, 83–105.

Centers for Disease Control and Prevention (2012) 'Prevalence of autism spectrum disorders: Autism and Developmental Disabilities Monitoring Network, 14 sites, United States, 2008.' *Centers for Disease Control's Morbidity and Mortality Weekly Report*, 30 March.

Centers for Disease Control and Prevention (2013) 'Adverse Childhood Experiences (ACE) Study: Data and statistics prevalence of individual adverse childhood experiences.' Available at www.cdc.gov/ace/prevalence.htm (accessed April 2013).

Craft, M.J. and Craft, A. (1987) *Sex and the Mentally Handicapped.* London: Routledge.

Cronch, L.E., Viljoen, J.L. and Hansen, D.J. (2006) 'Forensic interviewing in child sexual abuse cases: Current techniques and future directions.' *Aggression and Violent Behavior 11*, 3, 195–207.

Dahlgren, S. and Dahlgren Sandberg, A. (2008) 'Referential communication in children with autism spectrum disorder.' *Autism 12*, 4, 335–348.

Department for Children, Schools and Families (2009) *National Curriculum. Fourth Report of Session 2008–09. Volume 1.* London: DCSF. Available at www.educationengland.org.uk/documents/pdfs/2009_CSFC_nationalcurriculum.pdf (accessed June 2013).

Department for Education and Employment (2000) *Sex and Relationship Guidance.* London: DfEE. Available at www.education.gov.uk (accessed April 2013).

Department for Education and Skills (DfES) (2002) *Education Act 2002.* London: HMSO. Available at www.legislation.gov.uk/ukpga/2002/32/pdfs/ukpga_20020032_en.pdf (accessed August 2013).

Department of Health (2013) *Transforming Care: A National Response to Winterbourne View Hospital.* London: DOH.

Department of Health and Department for Children, Schools and Families (2007) *A Transition Guide for All Services: Key Information for Professionals about the Transition Process for Disabled Young People.* London: DH and DCSF. Available at http://dera.ioe.ac.uk/8105/1/transition_guide.pdf (accessed April 2013).

Department of Health and Department for Children, Schools and Families (2008) *Transition: Moving on Well.* London: DH and DCSF. Available at www.bacdis.org.uk/policy/documents/transition_moving-on-well.pdf (accessed April 2013).

Department of Health and Home Office (2000) *No Secrets: Guidance on Developing and Implementing Multi-agency Policies and Procedures to Protect Vulnerable Adults from Abuse.* London: Department of Health and Home Office.

Dominick, K.C., Davis, N.O., Lainhart, J., Tager-Flusberg, H. and Folstein, S. (2007) 'Atypical behaviors in children with autism and children with a history of language impairment.' *Research in Developmental Disabilities 28*, 2, 145–162.

Eaves, L.C. and Ho, H.H. (1996) 'Brief report: Stability and change in cognitive and behavioural characteristics of autism through childhood.' *Journal of Autism and Developmental Disorders 26*, 5, 557–569.

Edelson, S. (2011) 'Autism, puberty and the possibility of seizures.' *Autism Research Unit.* Available at www.autism.com/ind_puberty_seizures.asp (accessed February 2013).

Eggerding, C. (2010) 'Put sleep difficulties to bed: Advice for parents of children with autism.' Available at www.webmd.com/brain/autism/features/sleep-difficulties-parents-autism (accessed February 2013).

Emerson, E. (2001) *Challenging Behaviour: Analysis and Intervention in People with Learning Disabilities* (2nd edition). Cambridge: Cambridge University Press.

Everett, B. (2007) 'Ethically managing sexual activity in long-term care.' *Sexuality and Disability 25*, 1, 21–27.

Family Law Week (2011) *D Borough Council v AB (2011) EWHC 101 COP*. Available at www.familylawweek.co.uk/site.aspx?i=ed79322 (accessed April 2013).

Family Law Week (2012) *A Local Authority v H (2012) EWHC 49 (COP)*. Available at www.familylawweek.co.uk/site.aspx?i=ed96128 (accessed February 2013).

Family Planning Association (FPA) and Public Health Agency (2010) *Sexual Health and People with Learning Disabilities Factsheet*. Belfast: Family Planning Association.

Fegan, L., Rauch, A. and McCarthy, W. (1993) *Sexuality and People with Disability*. Baltimore, MD: Brookes.

Franklin, A. (2008) 'The participation of disabled children and young people in decision-making.' *Highlight 241*. London: National Children's Bureau.

Garbutt, R. (2008) 'Sex and relationships for people with learning disabilities: A challenge for parents and professionals.' *Mental Health and Learning Disabilities and Practice 5*, 2, 266–277.

Gerhardt, P. (2006) 'Sexuality instruction and autism spectrum disorders.' *Autism-Asperger's Digest*, November–December.

Gerressu, M., Mercer, C.H., Graham, C.A., Wellings, K. and Johnson, A.M. (2008) 'Prevalence of masturbation and associated factors in a British national probability survey.' *Archive of Sexual Behaviour 37*, 2, 266–278.

Gill, K. and Hough, S. (2007) *Sexuality Training, Education and Therapy in the Healthcare Environment: Taboo, Avoidance, Discomfort or Ignorance?* London: Sage.

Goldman, R.L. (1994) 'Children and youth with intellectual disabilities: Targets for sexual abuse.' *International Journal of Disability, Development, and Education 41*, 2, 89–102.

Gray, C. (2000) *The New Social Story Book (Illustrated Edition)*. Arlington, TX: Future Horizons.

Grieve, A., McLaren, S. and Lindsay, W. (2006) 'An evaluation of research and training resources for the sex education of people with moderate to severe learning disabilities.' *British Journal of Learning Disabilities 35*, 1, 30–37.

Hale, C.M. and Tager-Flusberg, H. (2005) 'Social communication in children with autism: The relationship between theory of mind and discourse development.' *Autism 9*, 2, 157–178.

Haracopos, D. and Pedersen, L. (1992) 'Sexuality and autism: Danish report.' *Autism UK Independent*. Available at www.autismuk.com/?page_id=1293 (accessed April 2013).

Hatton, S. and Tector, A. (2010) 'Sexuality and relationship education for young people with autistic spectrum disorder: Curriculum change and staff support.' *British Journal of Special Education 37*, 2, 69–76.

Henderson, M. (2012) 'I love my disabled child – but I'd give my life to make her normal.' *Daily Mail*, 28 November. Available at www.dailymail.co.uk/femail/article-2239513/The-mother-severely-autistic-girl-makes-painfully-honest-confession.html (accessed February 2013).

Hinsburger, D. (1994) 'Masturbation: A consultation for those who support individuals with developmental disabilities.' *Canadian Journal of Human Sexuality 3*, 3, 278–282.

HM Treasury and Department for Education and Skills (2007) *Aiming High for Disabled Children: Better Support for Families*. Available at www.education.gov.uk/publications/eOrderingDownload/PU213.pdf (accessed April 2013).

Hollomotz, A. (2011) *Learning Difficulties and Sexual Vulnerability: A Social Approach*. London: Jessica Kingsley Publishers.

Howard, R. and Hendy, S. (2004) 'The sterilisation of women with learning disabilities – Some points for consideration.' *British Journal of Developmental Disabilities 50*, 99, 133–141.

Howard-Barr, E.M., Rienzo, B.A., Morgan Pigg Jr, R., and James, D. (2005) 'Teacher beliefs, professional preparation and practices regarding exceptional students and sexuality education.' *Journal of School Health 75*, 3, 99–104.

James, E.L. (2011) *Fifty Shades of Grey*. New York: Knopf Doubleday.

Johnson, K., Frawley, P., Hillier, L. and Harrison, L. (2002) 'Living safer sexual lives: Research and action.' *Tizard Learning Review 7*, 1, 4–9.

Kaeser, F. (1996) 'Developing a philosophy of masturbation training for persons with severe or profound mental retardation.' *Sexuality and Disability 14*, 4, 295–308.

Kalyva, E. (2010) 'Teachers' perspectives of the sexuality of children with autism spectrum disorders.' *Research in Autism Spectrum Disorders 4*, 3, 433–437.

Keeling, J. (2006) 'Guides to safe and happy living.' *Times Educational Supplement TES Extra*, June.

Kendall-Tackett, K.A., Williams, L.M. and Finkelhor, D. (1993) 'Impact of sexual abuse on children: A review and synthesis of recent empirical studies.' *Psychological Bulletin 113*, 1, 164–180.

Koller, R.A. (2000) 'Sexuality and adolescents with autism.' *Sexuality and Disability 18*, 2, 125–135.

Kübler-Ross, E. (1969 [updated 2005]) *On Grief and Grieving: Finding the Meaning of Grief Through the Five Stages of Loss*. New York: Simon & Schuster.

Laumann, E.O. (1994) *The Social Organization of Sexuality: Sexual Practices in the United States*. Chicago, IL: University of Chicago Press.

Lesselliers, J. (1999) 'A right to sexuality?' *British Journal of Learning Disabilities 27*, 4, 137–140.

Lesselliers, J. and Van Hove, G. (2002) 'Barriers to development of intimate relationships and the expression of sexuality among people with developmental disabilities: Their perceptions.' *Research and Practice for Person with Severe Disabilities 27*, 1, 69–81.

Lockhart, K., Guerin, S., Shanahan, S. and Coyle, K. (2009) 'Defining "sexualized challenging behaviour" in adults with intellectual disabilities.' *Journal of Policy and Practice in Intellectual Disabilities 6*, 4, 293–301.

McCabe, M.P. (1999) 'Sexual knowledge, experience and feelings among people with disability.' *Sexuality and Disability 17*, 2, 157–170.

McCarthy, M. (1999) *Sexuality and Women with Learning Disabilities*. London: Jessica Kingsley Publishers.

McConkey, R., McAuley, P., Simpson, L. and Collins, S. (2007) 'The male workforce in intellectual disability services.' *Journal of Policy and Practice in Intellectual Disabilities 4*, 3, 186–193.

McGovern, C.W. and Sigman, M. (2004) 'Continuity and change from early childhood to adolescence in autism.' *Journal of Child Psychology and Psychiatry 46*, 4, 401–408.

McVilly, K. (2007) *Positive Behaviour Support for People with Intellectual Disability: Evidence-based Practice, Promoting Quality of Life*. Sydney, Australia: Australian Society for the Study of Intellectual Disability.

Manasco, H. and Manasco, K. (2012) *An Exceptional Children's Guide to Touch: Teaching Social and Physical Boundaries to Kids*. London: Jessica Kingsley Publishers.

Mansell, S., Sobsey, D. and Moskal, R. (1998) 'Clinical findings among sexually abused children with and without developmental disabilities.' *Mental Retardation 36*, 1, 12–22.

Marshall, W.L., Anderson, D. and Fernandez, Y.M. (1999) *Cognitive Behavioural Treatment of Sexual Offenders*. Chichester: Wiley.

Masters, W.H. and Johnson, V.E. (1988) *Sex and Human Loving*. Delhi: Jaico.

Merrick, M.T., Litrownik, A.J., Everson, M.D. and Cox, C.E. (2008) 'Beyond sexual abuse: The impact of other maltreatment experiences on sexualized behaviors.' *Child Maltreatment 13*, 2, 122–132.

Mitchell, J.E. and Popkin, M.K. (1983) 'Antidepressant drug therapy and sexual function in men: A review.' *Journal of Clinical Psychopharmacology 3*, 2, 76–79.

Morris, J. (2001) *'That Kind of Life?' Social Exclusion and Young Disabled People with High Levels of Support Needs.* London: Scope UK.

Murphy, N. and Young, P. (2005) 'Sexuality in children and adolescents with developmental disabilities.' *Pediatrics 18*, 1, 398–403.

Nario-Redmond, M.R. (2010) 'Cultural stereotypes of disabled and non-disabled men and women: Consensus for global category representations and diagnostic domains.' *British Journal of Social Psychology 49*, 3, 471–488.

Nind, M. and Hewett, D. (2001) *A Practical Guide to Intensive Interaction.* London: David Fulton.

OFSTED (2006) *Sex and Relationships Education in Schools. London: Office for Standards in Education, Children's Services and Skills.* Available at www.ofsted.gov.uk/resources/sex-and-relationships-education-schools (accessed July 2013).

Parsons, T. (1951) *The Social System.* London: Routledge.

Patti, P.J. (1995) 'Sexuality and sexual expression in persons with mental retardation.' *SIECUS Report 23*, 17–23.

Premack, D.G. and Woodruff, G. (1978) 'Does the chimpanzee have a theory of mind?' *Behavioral and Brain Sciences 1*, 4, 515–526.

Ray, F., Marks, C. and Bray-Garretson, H. (2004) 'Challenges to treating adolescents with Asperger's syndrome who are sexually abusive.' *Sexual Addiction and Compulsivity 11*, 265–285.

Realmuto, G.M. and Ruble, L.A. (1999) 'Sexual behaviours in autism: Problems of definition and management.' *Journal of Autism and Developmental Disorders 29*, 2, 121–127.

Reiter, L. (1989) 'Sexual orientation, sexual identity and the question of choice.' *Clinical Social Work Journal 17*, 2, 138–150.

Ruble, L.A. and Dalrymple, N.J. (1993) 'Social/sexual awareness of persons with autism: A parental perspective.' *Archives of Sexual Behavior 22*, 3, 229–240.

Russell, D.E.H. (1998) *Dangerous Relationships: Pornography, Misogyny, and Rape.* Thousand Oaks, CA: Sage.

Schopler, E., Reicher, R. and Renner, B. (1986) *The Childhood Autism Rating Scale (CARS): For Diagnostic Screening and Classification of Autism.* New York: Irvington.

Scott, S., Jackson, S. and Backett-Milburn, K. (1998) 'Swings and roundabouts: Risk anxiety and the everyday worlds of children.' *Sociology 32*, 4, 689–705.

Shakespeare, T., Gillespie-Sells, K. and Davies, D. (1996) *The Sexual Politics of Disability: Untold Desires.* London: Cassell.

Simpson, A., Lafferty, A. and McConkey, R. (2006) *Out of the Shadows: A Report of the Sexual Health and Wellbeing of People with Learning Disabilities in Northern Ireland.* Belfast: Family Planning Association.

Sinson, J.C. (1995) *Care in the Community for Young People with Learning Disabilities: The Client's Voice.* London: Jessica Kingsley Publishers.

Social Care Association (undated) *Adult Relationships for People with Learning Difficulties.* New Malden, UK: Social Care Association.

St John's Ambulance Service (2013) 'Seizures in adults.' Available at www.sja.org.uk/sjafirst-aid-advice/head-injuries-and-seizures/seizures.aspx (accessed April 2013).

Stanfield, J. (undated) 'Circles Curriculum.' Available at www.stanfield.com/products/family-life-relationships/social-skills-circles-curriculum-intimacy-relationships (accessed April 2013).

Sterling-Turner, H.E. and Jordan, S. (2007) 'Interventions addressing transition difficulties for individuals with autism.' *Psychology in the Schools 44*, 7, 681–690.

Stokes, M. and Kaur, A. (2005) 'High-functioning autism and sexuality: A parental perspective.' *Autism 9*, 3, 266–289.

Stokes, M., Newton, N. and Kaur, A. (2007) 'Stalking, and social and romantic functioning among adolescents and adults with autism spectrum disorder.' *Journal of Autism and Developmental Disorders 37*, 10, 1969–1986.

Sullivan, A. and Caterino, L.C. (2008) 'Addressing the sexuality and sex education of individuals with autism spectrum disorders.' *Education and Treatment of Children 31*, 3, 381–394.

Sullivan, P.M. and Knutson, J.F. (2000) 'Maltreatment and disabilities: A population-based epidemiological study.' *Child Abuse and Neglect 24*, 10, 1257–1273.

Swango-Wilson, A. (2008) 'Caregiver perception of sexual behaviors of individuals with intellectual disabilities.' *Sexuality and Disability 26*, 2, 75–81.

Szollos, A.A. and McCabe, M.P. (1995) 'The sexuality of people with mild intellectual disability: Perceptions of clients and caregivers.' *Australia and New Zealand Journal of Developmental Disabilities 20*, 3, 205–222.

Tang, S.S.S., Freyd, J.J. and Wang, M. (2007) 'What do we know about gender in the disclosure of child sexual abuse?' *Journal of Psychological Trauma 6*, 4, 1–26.

Tarnai, B. and Wolfe, P. (2008) 'Social stories for sexuality education for persons with autism/pervasive developmental disorder.' *Sexuality and Disability 26*, 1, 29–36.

Tissot, C. (2009) 'Establishing a sexual identity: Case studies of learners with Autism and learning difficulties.' *Autism 13*, 6, 551–566.

Travers, J. and Tincani, M. (2010) 'Sexuality education for individuals with autism spectrum disorders: Critical issues and decision making guidelines.' *Education and Training in Autism and Developmental Disabilities 45*, 2, 284–293.

Valios, N. (2002) 'Learning to love safely.' *Community Care 1415*, 32–33.

Van Bourgondien, M., Reichle, N. and Palmer, A. (1997) 'Sexual behavior in adults with autism.' *Journal of Autism and Developmental Disorders 27*, 2, 113–125.

Vaughn, B.J., White, R., Johnston, S. and Dunlap, G. (2005) 'Positive behavior support as a family-centered endeavor.' *Journal of Positive Behavior Interventions 7*, 1, 55–58.

Walker-Hirsch, L. and Champagne, M.P. (1991) 'The Circles Concept: Social competence in special education.' *Education Leadership 49*, 1, 65. Available at www.ascd.org/ASCD/pdf/journals/ed_lead/el_199109_walker-hirsch.pdf (accessed June 2013).

Watson, S., Venema, T., Molloy, W. and Reich, M. (2002) 'Sexual Rights and Individuals Who Have a Developmental Disability.' In D. Griffiths, D. Richards, P. Fedoroff and S. Watson (eds) *Ethical Dilemmas: Sexuality and Developmental Disability.* Kingston, NY: NADD Press.

Wilson, N., Parmenter, T., Stancliffe, R. and Shuttleworth, R. (2009) *Conditionally Sexual: Constructing the Sexual Health Needs of Men and Teenage Boys with Moderate to Profound Intellectual Disability.* Sydney, NSW: University of Sydney.

Wing, L. (1981) 'Sex ratios in early childhood autism and related conditions.' *Psychiatry Research 5*, 2, 129–137.

Wolfensberger, W. (1972) *The Principle of Normalization in Human Services.* Toronto: National Institute on Mental Retardation.

World Health Organization (1992) *International Classification of Diseases* (ICD-10). Geneva: WHO.

World Health Organization (2004) 'Sexual health – a new focus for WHO.' *Progress in Reproductive Health Research 64*. Available at www.redactivas.org/media/uploads/public/1_Sexual_health_a_new_focus_for_WHO.pdf (accessed April 2013).

Resources

CDs/DVDs

Baron-Cohen, S. (2004) *Mind Reading: The Interactive Guide to Emotions*. CD-Rom. London: Jessica Kingsley Publishers
Exercises to learn about respecting others.

FPA (2011) *Talking Together…about Sex and Relationships*. London: FPA

FPA (2011) *Talking Together…about Growing Up*. London: FPA
Two practical resource books and DVDs by the Family Planning Association for schools and parents working with young disabled people with learning disabilities.
www.fpa.org.uk

Hingsburger, D. (2000) *Hand Made Love: A Guide for Teaching about Male Masturbation*. Barrie, Ontario: Diverse City Press
The book and DVD explore the myths surrounding masturbation and suggest it can be a way of learning about sex and discusses masturbation in terms of health and pleasure.
www.diverse-city.com/dvds

Hingsburger, D. and Haar, S. (1999) *Finger Tips: A Guide for Teaching about Female Masturbation*. Barrie, Ontario: Diverse City Press
www.diverse-city.com/dvds

Life Support Productions (undated) *The New Guide to Relationships and Sex*. Life Support Productions
A DVD for young people facing transition.
Tel: 020 7723 7520
www.lifesupportproductions.co.uk

Life Support Productions (undated) *You, Your Body and Sex*. Life Support Productions
A comprehensive sex education guide for young people with learning disabilities on DVD.
Tel: 020 7723 7520
www.lifesupportproductions.co.uk

Demonstration Models

Anatomically Correct Cloth Dolls
www.bodysense.org.uk

Ejaculating Penis and Condom Demonstrator
For simulators, anatomical models and charts for clinical skills and training.
Tel: 01795 479787
www.adam-rouilly.co.uk

Wendy
An anatomically correct 3D latex model showing internal and external female
genitalia available in three skin colours.
www.bodysense.org.uk

Pictorial Books and Booklets

Craft, A. and Dixon, H. (2006) *Picture Yourself*
A series of picture cards with teaching notes covering changes during puberty,
public and private behaviours, masturbation, using condoms, using public
toilets and making relationships.
www.bodysense.org.uk

Feeling Grown Up
A series of booklets for young people with autism and learning difficulties:
• Menstruation at Home
• Menstruation at the Disco
• Masturbation – Male
• Masturbation – Female
• Wet Dreams
• Use of Public Toilets
Tel: 0115 915 3265
Email: admin@oakfield.nottingham.sch.uk

Gaskell (various dates) *Books Beyond Words*. Gaskell Publications
A series of pictorial books which use pictures to enable explanation of events and
issues for people with learning difficulties. Titles include:
• *Falling in Love*
• *Looking After My Balls*
• *Loving Each Other Safely*
• *Keeping Healthy 'Down Below'*
Tel: 020 7235 2351 (ext: 146)
www.rcpsych.ac.uk/publications/gaskellbooks.aspx

Growing Up, Sex and Relationships
A series of booklets to support young disabled people, available as free downloads
and podcasts for the following groups:
• Teachers

- Young disabled people
- Parents

Tel: 0808 808 3555

www.cafamily.org.uk

I Change My Pad

Booklet reminding females with learning difficulties when and how to change a sanitary pad. Illustrated with photographs which show how to remove and throw away a pad, how to put a fresh one in place and a reminder to wash hands.

www.bodysense.org.uk

Manasco, H. and Manasco, K. (2012) *An Exceptional Children's Guide to Touch: Teaching Social and Physical Boundaries to Kids.* London: Jessica Kingsley Publishers

Jessica Kingsley Publishers is an independent publisher of accessible books that make a difference, specialising in Asperger syndrome, autism, social work, arts therapies, education and similar fields.

www.jkp.com

Now They Are Growing Up

A series of booklets for parents about:

- Menstruation
- Male Masturbation
- Female Masturbation
- HIV/AIDS
- Protecting Your Child
- A Planned, Dependent Life and Sexuality
- Loss

Tel: 0115 915 3265

Email: admin@oakfield.nottingham.sch.uk

Pictorial Cards

CHANGE (various dates) *Sex and Relationship Pack*

Book 1: *Friendships and Relationships*

Book 2: *Sex and Masturbation*

Book 3: *Safe Sex and Contraception*

Book 4: *Lesbian, Gay, Bisexual and Trans*

Book 5: *Sexual Abuse*

CHANGE pictures can be paid for and downloaded:

www.changepeople.co.uk

Health Edco (undated) *How to Perform Breast Self-Examination (BSE)*

A chart with clear pictures.

www.healthedco.co.uk

How It Is: An Image Vocabulary for Children about Feelings, Rights and Safety, Personal Care and Sexuality
Comprehensive cards of images that many communication systems miss.
www.howitis.org.uk

Makaton Books of Signs and Symbols
Books about sex education and personal, social and health education.
www.makaton.org.uk

Teaching Packs

Bodyworks
A framework which aims to develop awareness of 'self ' through practical experiences. The body is broken down into four sections and suggested teaching activities are arranged in these sections to provide experience and/or promote awareness of issues around the following themes:

- Health and hygiene
- Appearance
- Independence
- Protection
- Physical care
- Social and sexual awareness

Tel: 0115 915 3265
Email: admin@oakfield.nottingham.sch.uk

Brook (2011) *Living Your Life*. Brook Publications
A comprehensive publication for those working with young people with special educational needs and learning difficulties. It helps teachers and youth workers to design, deliver and evaluate a programme of sex and relationships education and includes seven modules covering group-building; the physical self; emotions; relationships; sexual expression; public and private; being healthy and staying safe.
Tel: 02476 545557
Email: brook@adc-uk.com

Dodd, K., Jones, K., Liddiard, H. and Stroud, J. (2007) *Exploring Sexual and Social Understanding: An Illustrated Pack Designed for Working with People with Learning Disabilities*. Kidderminster: BILD Publications
An illustrated pack by the British Institute of Learning Disabilities (BILD), designed for working with people with learning disabilities as a visual resource which can be used to assess sexual knowledge and capacity to consent to sex. The pack includes a capacity to consent assessment form.
www.bild.org.uk

Hart, P. and Douglas-Scott, S. (2005) *Batteries Not Included – A Sexuality Resource Pack for Working with People with Complex Communication Support Needs*. Glasgow: Common Knowledge
A sexuality resource pack outlining challenges of sexuality teaching and people with complex communication support needs. It includes a sensuality toolkit.

Keeling, J. (2005) *Growing and Learning about Sexual Health*. Growing and Learning
   Three books, exercises and cards by Jane Keeling to support parents and health
   educators of young people with learning disabilities:
   Book 1: *A Parents' and Carers' Toolkit*
   Book 2: *A Parents' and Carers' Toolkit – Young Men*
   Book 3: *A Parents' and Carers' Toolkit – Young Women*
   www.growingandlearning.co.uk

Periods: A Practical Guide
   A training pack to provide women with learning difficulties with a visual
   guide to sanitary protection while menstruating. It is a book with a CD for
   health educators.
   www.bodysense.org.uk

Speirs, F. (undated) *A PSHE Programme for Learners with Autistic Spectrum Disorders*
   Fiona Speirs is an education consultant specialising in working with children
   and adults with special needs, their families and those who support in a
   professional capacity.
   www.fionaspeirs.co.uk

Textbooks

Blake, S. and Katrak, Z. (2002) *Faith, Values and Sex and Relationships Education*.
   London: National Children's Bureau
   A book which examines key values and beliefs around sexuality. It includes
   sexual orientation, masturbation, pornography, sexual relationships outside
   marriage and contraception.
   *http://ncb.org.uk/media/244761/faith__values_and_sex_and_relationships_
   education.pdf*

Fanstone, C. and Andrews, S. (2009) *Learning Disabilities, Sex and the Law: A
   Practical Guide*. London: FPA
   A comprehensive examination of the Sexual Offences Act 2003 and how it
   impacts on people with learning disabilities.
   Tel: 0845 122 8600
   www.fpa.org.uk

Useful Agencies

BodySense
Organisation established to develop and make available innovative teaching resources
that respond to the sex education needs of young people of all abilities.
www.bodysense.org.uk

British Institute of Learning Disabilities (BILD)
BILD helps you to support people with learning disabilities to make their own
decisions and choices about their lives.
www.bild.org.uk

Brook

Brook gives free and confidential advice on sexual health for the under 25s.
Tel: 0808 802 1234
www.brook.org.uk/home

CEREBRA

A charity helping to improve the lives of children with brain-related conditions through research, education and directly supporting the children and their carers.
www.cerebra.org.uk

Challenging Behaviour Foundation

A leading national human rights organisation led by disabled people, providing many different resources and support.
www.changepeople.co.uk

Common Knowledge

This produces award-winning accessible online learning for people with learning difficulties.
www.ckuk.org.uk

Contact a Family

Organisation supporting families with disabled children.
www.cafamily.org.uk

Diverse City Press

A small publishing company which aims to provide educational materials for people with intellectual disabilities and their parents and carers.
www.diverse-city.com

Family Planning Association (FPA)

FPA offers information, advice and support on sexual health, sex and relationships to everyone in the UK, including:
Desire and Pleasure
Online shops for a range of sex toys, accessories and games to enhance sexual pleasure and well-being.
www.fpa.org.uk

Health Edco UK

Organisation that offers a variety of packages to enable practising self-examination of testicles and breasts. Kits come with DVD flip chart and model.
www.healthedco.co.uk

Image in Action

Image in Action believes that people with disabilities have a right to information and understanding about sexuality. For over 25 years it has been putting that belief into action, developing effective methods and creating new ways of making complex issues safe and accessible.
www.imageinaction.org

Intensive Interaction Institute
This promotes the use of intensive interaction as an approach to severe autism and learning disabilities.
www.intensiveinteraction.co.uk

National Autistic Society
NAS is a charity for people with autism and their families, providing information, support, services and training.
www.autism.org.uk

PSHE (Personal, Social, Health and Economic Education) Association
This is the subject association for all professionals working in PSHE education.
www.pshe-association.org.uk

The Son-Rise Programme
Son-Rise is a home-based play programme for children on the autism spectrum, using the concept of 'joining'.
www.autismtreatmentcenter.org

Young Carers
Young Carers is part of the Carers Trust, the Princess Royal Trust for Carers, which supports young people who care for someone with a disability at home.
www.carers.org

Subject Index

Author Index